AFSPA
& Human Rights Violation:
Analytical findings of Ukhrul District, Manipur

Dr. Depend Kazingmei

BLUEROSE PUBLISHERS
India | U.K.

Copyright © Dr Depend Kazingmei 2024

All rights reserved by author. No part of this publication may be reproduced, stored in a retrieval system or transmitted in any form or by any means, electronic, mechanical, photocopying, recording or otherwise, without the prior permission of the author. Although every precaution has been taken to verify the accuracy of the information contained herein, the publisher assumes no responsibility for any errors or omissions. No liability is assumed for damages that may result from the use of information contained within.

BlueRose Publishers takes no responsibility for any damages, losses, or liabilities that may arise from the use or misuse of the information, products, or services provided in this publication.

For permissions requests or inquiries regarding this publication,
please contact:

BLUEROSE PUBLISHERS
www.BlueRoseONE.com
info@bluerosepublishers.com
+91 8882 898 898
+4407342408967

ISBN: 978-93-5628-697-9

Cover design: Aveek
Typesetting:Rohit

First Edition: February 2024

Acknowledgement

While several people have been instrumental in writing this book. This book wouldn't have existed without their contribution and insight of them.

First and foremost, I would like to thank the Almighty God for His grace, strength, knowledge, and forever lending hands in completing this book. I am deeply grateful to the NPMHR Ukhrul Unit and Mr. Phungyo Hungyo for their assistance in finding the documents. My heartfelt appreciation goes to all the field assistants who played a crucial role in collecting data and filling out the questionnaire.

I cannot find befitting words to express my deep sense of gratitude to my Uncle Mr. Langzar Kazingmei and other well-wishers for the financial help. I am indeed grateful to all my friends for the unending moral support, sharing of ideas, and encouragement in completing this book. I would like to extend my sincere thanks to all the individuals, CSOs, and Ukhrul Police Department for their support and for providing valuable information.

Last but not least, I would like to share a word of God that has been an inspiration and a motivational mechanism for me during my undulating journey of writing this book. It's from the Bible, Psalm 23:1: 'The Lord is my Shepherd; I shall not want.'

~ Dr. Depend Kazingmei

Preface

India is the largest democratic country, yet the value of human rights has been immensely neglected. The constitution appears to be vague for many of the citizens because their rights are deprived by the Armed Forces Special Powers Act (AFSPA), and they are both directly and indirectly ruled by the ruthless act. The AFSPA has extremely violated several human rights to a large extent and condoned extra-judicial killings in the state. Even though the Armed Forces are accountable for the violations and crimes committed, they are safeguarded by the Constitution. This has created a new category of Indian citizens, who are considered "killable people" and "rape-able women," according to Babloo Loitongbam, a human rights activist and lawyer. In the space of 33 years, a concrete record of at least 1,528 extrajudicial executions of civilians has been documented. In protest to repeal this draconian law, the Iron Lady of Manipur, Irom Sharmila, has continued hunger strikes for 16 long years but has been unable to abrogate it.

As widely known, the incident in the Oinam village (Senapati district) in 1987, during which the Assam Rifles launched 'Operation Bluebird,' lasted for four months and involved inhuman torture, grouping of villages, forced labor, sexual harassment, rape, manslaughter, murder, looting and theft, desecration of the church, arson, illegal detentions, and arrests. Around thirty villages experienced the unjust bitterness of the Armed Forces. Every child of Oinam has a story to tell when recounting the nightmarish tale of 'Operation Blue Bird 1987'. This incident left an indelible mark with its unjust and bitter actions, creating a lasting imprint on the collective memory of the community. The memories of the hardships endured during this operation persist, and the acknowledged impact on their lives resonates. These collective narratives contribute to a broader understanding of the historical context, fostering awareness, empathy, and remembrance for generations to come.

The recent infamous incident in Oting on 4th December 2021, where fake encounters by Army commandos led to indiscriminate firing on the vehicle carrying miners without confirming identification, resulted in the tragic deaths of six innocent civilians. The other two individuals, who were seriously injured, luckily survived and provided crucial evidence that might have otherwise been distorted. The security forces attempted to cover up the wanton killings, purportedly by covering the bodies with a tarpaulin, which infuriated the civilians, leading to further violence and the loss of life of six more villagers and a jawan of the Assam Rifles. The trials of these cases have been proceeding at a slow pace, leaving the matter still unresolved to date. The unbridled power provided by the Armed Forces Special Powers Act (AFSPA) to the security forces does create conditions for heavy-handedness.

AFSPA is all about providing protection to the Armed Forces and indirectly encouraging them to commit human rights violations. When a state is declared a disturbed area by the central government, AFSPA is enforced in order to bring normal functioning to the broken government. The motives and objectives of imposing AFSPA are to restore normalcy by deploying the Armed Forces. However, its indefinite deployment has unfortunately resulted in the violation of human rights and loaded strife in the community. In a democratic country, human rights have to be respected and even any Act or deployment of the Armed Forces should be for a limited period.

The Central and State governments have a moral obligation to protect and provide security to the people of Manipur, and yet they have failed to do so. Poor governance and insurgency are not the ultimate causes for imposing AFSPA, but there is some hidden agenda that the local populace is not aware of. Unfortunately, in the district of Ukhrul, it is quite the opposite of the constitutional rights given for the protection of citizens. The district was considered a 'disturbed area' even before AFSPA was imposed in the whole state on 8th September 1980. The fact is, even if there is peace and harmony in the state, it is always considered disturbed due to hostility. Taking advantage of this, gross human rights violations have been committed for decades. Several protests and rallies have been staged but have gone unnoticed by the Central and State governments, leaving much agitation and protests in vain.

The information and statistical findings are sourced from my Ph.D. thesis, conferred in 2020, which forms the basis of a book focusing on the inference of public opinion. This publication is centered on understanding public sentiment, with a primary emphasis on formulating constructive solutions derived from input provided by various stakeholders and civil society organizations.

The overarching objective is to nurture a deeper understanding between the Tangkhul community and the Armed Forces. Consequently, the book is poised to make a substantial impact, not only influencing the Armed Forces and the residents of Ukhrul but also contributing positively to the broader well-being of the state of Manipur as a whole.

Justice delayed is justice denied.

~ William E. Gladstone

Dedicated to the victims of human rights violations, especially

Achon Rose Ningshen

&

Achon Luingamla Muinao.

Declaration

This book is not intended to incite sedition, threaten national security, or disrupt national unity.

The author sincerely apologizes for any unintended misconceptions caused.

CONTENTS

1. HUMAN RIGHTS ORIGIN AND DEVELOPMENT IN INDIA 1
2. UNIVERSAL DECLARATION OF HUMAN RIGHTS 8
3. NATIONAL HUMAN RIGHTS COMMISSION 13
4. UNIVERSAL DECLARATION OF HUMAN RIGHTS AND INDIAN CONSTITUTION 15
5. MANIPUR HUMAN RIGHTS COMMISSION 18
6. CONSTITUTIONAL RIGHTS FOR TRIBALS 21
7. ARMED FORCES SPECIAL POWER ACT (AFSPA) 1958 24
8. NATURE OF HUMAN RIGHTS VIOLATION 30
9. NAGA PEOPLE'S MOVEMENT FOR HUMAN RIGHTS (NPMHR) 32
10. TANGKHUL NAGA 34
11. METHODOLOGY 39
12. HUMAN RIGHTS VIOLATION IN THE SELECTED VILLAGES 42
13. HUMAN RIGHTS VIOLATION INCIDENTS IN UKHRUL DISTRICT 50
14. INCIDENTS OF ATTACK/ AMBUSH IN UKHRUL DISTRICT, 2007 - 2017 86
15. IMPACT OF ARMED FORCES SPECIAL POWER ACT (AFSPA) 89
16. STATE GOVERNMENT ACTION AGAINST HUMAN RIGHTS VIOLATION 126
17. CIVIL SOCIETY ORGANIZATIONS' INTERVENTION IN HUMAN RIGHTS VIOLATION 130
18. HYPOTHESIS TESTING 143
19. CASE STUDY 148
20. ANALYTICAL FINDINGS 165
21. SUGGESTIONS 173

REFERENCES *179*
ABBREVIATIONS *185*
APPENDIX *188*

1

HUMAN RIGHTS ORIGIN AND DEVELOPMENT IN INDIA

Historical Foundations of Human Rights

The protection of human rights can be traced back to the early Babylonian laws. The Babylonian King Hammurabi produced a set of laws for his people known as "Hammurabi's Code." These laws encompassed provisions for fair wages, safety, protection of property, and the necessity of essential charges for trials. Similarly, the Hittite laws, Assyrian Laws, and the Dharma of the Vedic period in Ancient India established various standards of rights to ensure that every person was respected by others. Every major religion in the world has a humanist perspective that supports human rights in their teachings regardless of their differences in practices.

Human rights are deeply rooted in philosophical concepts such as "Natural Law" and "Natural Rights." The ideas of natural rights found recognition among Roman and certain Greek philosophers, with one of the early advocates for universal standards of ethical conduct being Plato (427-348 BC). Roman jurist Ulpian expressed the concept of natural law as that which "nature and the State assure to all human beings." According to this perspective, foreigners were to be treated in the same manner as co-patriots. This law was essential for civilized manner wars.

"The Republic (400 BC)" proposed that the concept of universal truths should be recognized by everyone. In "Politics," Aristotle (384-322 B.C.) mentioned that justice, virtue, and rights change in accordance with different kinds of institutions and circumstances. Cicero (106-43 B.C.), a Roman statesman, also discussed the fundamentals of "Natural Law" and "Human Rights" in his writings, specifically in "The Laws (52 B.C.)."

Cicero argued that recognizing universal human rights law is essential, going beyond existing customary and civil laws.

One of the first individuals to endorse the concept of freedom of expression of opinion against the State was Sophocles (495-406 B.C.). Subsequently, the writings of the Christian philosopher St. Thomas Aquinas (1225-1274) emphasized "Natural Law" as a form of "divine law," suggesting that God revealed it to human beings for discovery through reasoning, with the intervention of God.

The "City-States of Greece" gave "equality before the law, freedom of speech, right to be elected to public office, right to vote, right to access to justice to their citizens, right to trade." Comparable rights were also protected by the Romans by the "Jus Civile" of the "Roman Law."[1] Therefore, the initial idea of human rights was found in the "Greco-Roman Natural Law" Doctrines of "Stoicism" which apprehend that a universal force spreads all creation and that any misconduct of a human being should not be spared from the judgment, it has to be deal as per the standard laws.

"The Magna Carta," also known as "Magna Charta" in Latin, consists of seventy subsections. As we know this law is not a full list of orders for liberty and civil rights, therefore, it cannot be stated as the initial point of Constitutional history that transfers the focus from the power of the State to human rights because it has preserved the principles of justice, liberty, fraternity and equality.[2] For the people of the United Kingdom, preserving these rights is a great accomplishment, nurturing them over the years as a symbol of hope for humanity. Despite limitations in the Magna Carta, especially under the clauses related to civil rights and liberties, it has had a profound impact on recognizing various individual rights. It empowers individuals to assert their rights from the State, establishing that the State must respect their opinions, and does not have the authority to interfere with the rights and freedom of individuals.

"The Magna Carta," granted by King John of England to English noblemen on June 15, 1215, was a response to the vehement opposition to the heavy taxation imposed during the 3rd Crusade and the ransom demanded for the

---

[1] P.N. Bhagwati, Seminar on Human Rights 7
[2] Justice A.M. Ahamadi, "inaugural Address on Fakhruddin Ali Ahamed Memorial Lecture on Democracy." Liberty and Changing Political Scenario, Date 29th July 2000, (New Delhi: GHAL B Institute Publication, 2000) 9.

release of Richard the Lionheart, who was captured by the Holy Roman Emperor Henry VI. The English noblemen resisted the imposition of burdensome taxes, and they demanded concessions regarding their rights, expressing their unwillingness for King John to continue ruling without such concessions. The overarching theme of the Magna Carta was to safeguard against arbitrary acts by the king, reflecting the noblemen's desire for limitations on royal power.

Consequently, property and land could no longer be arbitrarily seized, and taxes were prohibited from imposition without the consent of the general council. Additionally, judges were mandated to be knowledgeable about and respectful of the laws, and punishments could not be meted out without proper trials. As a result, the power of the king was no longer deemed supreme, in accordance with the principles of the Magna Carta. During the reign of "John's son, Henry Third," in 1216-17, the parliament reaffirmed the Magna Carta, and in the year 1297, Edward First also confirmed it in a modified form. Furthermore, in 1628, the Magna Carta was reinforced by the Petition of Rights, and later, in 1689, it was further solidified by the Bill of Rights, establishing a manifesto for Parliamentary supremacy over the Crown and providing a legal foundation for the Rule of Law in England. In summary, Hugo Grotius and St. Thomas Aquinas also emphasized in their writings that human beings are endowed with definite, eternal, and undeniable rights.

The concept of the "fundamental rights of man" is evident in the declarations and constitutional instruments of various states. Notably, the "Declaration of Independence" of the 13 American colonies in 1776 and the Constitution of the United States of America in 1787, amended in 1789, 1865, 1869, and 1919, articulated a set of rights. The "Virginia Declaration of Rights" proclaimed the inherent freedom and certain inalienable rights of all individuals. The French Declaration of the Rights of Man and of Citizen of 1789 inspired other European states to incorporate provisions in their laws to safeguard human rights. Consequently, declarations of fundamental rights were made in 1809 in Sweden, 1812 in Spain, 1814 in Norway, 1831 in Belgium, 1849 in Denmark, 1850 in Russia, and 1874 in Switzerland.

The words "Natural Rights" ultimately seem to be disapproval, but the idea of "Universal Rights" seems to be more specific. The term "The rights of man" seems to be not suitable, as the rights of women are included and yet it was not understood universally. In the year in 1947, Eleanor Roosevelt suggested the phrase "Rights of Man" be changed into "Human Rights". Even though Thomas Paine first used the words "Human Rights" and used in his English translation of the "French Declaration of the Rights of Man and Citizen (1789)".

In the "Classical Treatise - Civil Disobedience" by Henry David Thoreau, he expanded on this idea. Until the 19th and the beginning of the 20th century, any challenge to implement "Human Rights" was considered a violation of the idea of State sovereignty. Nevertheless, there were exceptions to this rule, such as the adoption of the Slavery Convention of 1926 and the establishment of the International Labour Organization in 1919. At the end of the First World War, the Covenant of the League of Nations was silent on the subject of human rights. Only with the realization of the value of human beings did the Institute of International Law make a declaration in 1929 about the "Rights of Man."

As a replacement to specify the rights of human beings, it has been laid down in the VI duties of the State. The public and official announcement of 1929 accepted the right of every person to liberty, prosperity, and life; the rights without any discrimination to sex, nationality, language, and race; the right of every person to practice in private or in public of any belief, faith, or religion. The public and official announcement is recognized as the best efforts towards the universalization of human rights. The 1940s marked a turning point for the traditional approach, particularly in the midst of severe human rights abuses during World War II in war-torn Europe. Horrific crimes against humanity were being committed, and there were absolute repressions of fundamental human rights.

The German Nazi leaders had established a system of absolute dictatorship and lawlessness. Their barbaric acts disregarded all human dignity and values within the territories they controlled, governed by their own rules. At this juncture, the reinstallation of the rights and liberty of the individual was recognized as the most necessary need for the formation of international peace and security. This theory was reflected in the public and official announcement made by American President Franklin D. Roosevelt on January 6, 1941, which later became known as the "Four Freedoms." Roosevelt declared in his message, "Freedom means the supremacy of human rights everywhere." In the Moscow Declaration of German

Atrocities on October 30, 1943, the United Kingdom, the United States, the Soviet Union, and France announced that the Germans would be held responsible for violating international law.

A lot of consultation and meetings were conducted prior to the establishment of the "United Nations" as an international body in 1945 "(United Nations Declaration, 1942; Moscow Declaration, 1943; Tehran Declaration, 1943; Dumbarton Oaks Conference, 1944 and San Francisco Conference, 1945)." A combined announcement was made by "President Franklin D. Roosevelt of the United States" and "Prime Minister Winston Churchill of the United Kingdom" on August 14, 1941, in a document recognized as the "Atlantic Charter." The announcement of the United Nations signed on January 1, 1942, in Washington was the earliest document using the term "Human Rights."[3] This document includes the signatories who were fighting against the Axis Powers recognized the need to "preserve human rights and justice in their own land as well as in other lands."[4]

Human Rights Development in India

Since the days of the Indus Valley Civilization, Indian culture has been the center of a diverse mixture of religion and cultural sources, which later spread out in the country over a period of time. According to the words of Jawaharlal Nehru, "an unbroken continuity between the most modern and the most ancient phases of Hindu thought extending over three thousand years."[5] Since the very beginning, the protection of human rights has been a main concern in the entire civilization. "The concept of the rights of man and other fundamental rights was not unknown to the people of earlier periods."[6] The "Assyrian laws in the Middle East" and the "Babylonian Laws," the "Dharma" of the "Vedic period in India" and the "jurisprudence of Lao-Tze" and "Confucius in China" have strongly recognized the value of human rights while tracing back the entire history of human civilization.

---

[3] H.O. Agarwal (2002), "International Law and Human Rights," 8th ed. (Allahabad: Central Law publications, 2002) 656.
[4] Declaration of the United Nations signed on January 1, 1942 at Washington, signed by 26 states, including USA, UK, USSR and China.
[5] Jawaharlar Nehru. "The Discovery of India, 2"ded. (New Delhl. JawaharlalNehru Memorial Fund, 1992) 88.
[6] Attar Chand, "Politics of Human Rights and Civil Liberties - A Global Survey" (Delhi: UDH Publishers, 1985) 45.

According to the perspective of Indians, they consider the individual, the society, and the universe as a complete organic whole. Everybody is considered as children of God and everyone is related to each other in one way or another and we are the family of the universe. In the words of Mahatma Gandhi, he said, "I do not want to think in terms of the whole world. My patriotism includes the good of mankind in general. Therefore, my service to India includes the services of humanity."[7]

Mahatma Phule was a social reformer, writer, and staunch advocate of human rights, who strived to create a new social order in India founded on justice, equality, fraternity, and liberty. He was the first to emphasize the importance of human rights and advocated for the rights of the underprivileged. He emphasized strongly on justice and there is no doubt that he was the pioneer of the Human Rights Movement in India. He worked relentlessly for Dalits' political, social, educational and economic rights. Believing that everyone had their own natural rights, he emerged as a militant advocate for the backward classes. He never gave up advocating for the downtrodden community and fearlessly strove to bring reform to Hindu society. He sought to remove feelings of inferiority from the minds of the backward class and wanted them to empower themselves.

Phule made powerful pleas to abolish untouchability and the entire caste-system, protesting against the unjust system under which millions of people had suffered for centuries. He not only emphasized social reform movements but also stressed on the equality of men and women to achieve true social justice and equality in society. He believed that there should be no discrimination between men and women in order to build a more equitable and just society. Through his efforts, Shudras became conscious of their inherent natural rights and started claiming them. He liberated not only the downtrodden community but also liberated women and empowered them to claim their place in society. His initiatives of widow remarriage and opposing child marriage gave new hope to many women. To his credit, he established an orphanage home, the first institution founded by a Hindu, to protect widows and orphans, provide them with hope and a chance to rebuild their lives. His contribution to society is a testament to his dedication to uplifting the marginalized and creating a more equitable society.

---

[7] Jawaharlal Nehru 420

According to Nagendra Singh, the Buddhist doctrine about non-violence, as per its teachings "is a humanitarian doctrine par excellence, dating back to the third century B.C".[8] Jainism also contained similar doctrines. As per the Bhagavad Gita, "he who has no ill will to any being, who is friendly and compassionate, who is free from egoism and self-sense and who is even-minded in pain and pleasure and patient" is beloved in the eyes of God.

It is also said that a person who has the nature and spirit of non-violence, liberty from anger, truth, rejection, feels contempt towards finding someone else's faults, shows compassion to others, abstains from the desire to possess others' belongings, tenderness, humility, and firmness are the qualities which humans need to have and it represents spirituality and divinity of human beings.[9] According to the historical perspective of ancient Bharat, it was affirmed without query that the value of human rights is visible in every religion, like in Islamic, ancient Hindu, and early Christian civilizations. Ancient leaders like Ashoka and Akbar cannot be removed from the chronology of human rights.[10]

---

[8] Nagendra Singh, "Enfor-ement of Human Rights" (Calcutta: Eastern LawHouse Pvt. Ltd, 1986) 7.
[9] S. Radhakrishnan (trans.) "The Bhagavadgita (London: George Allen andUnwin, 1958) 276."
[10] Yogesh K. Tyagi, "Third World Response to Human Rights," Indian Journal of International Law, Vo.21, No.1 (January -March 1981): 120-121.

2

UNIVERSAL DECLARATION OF HUMAN RIGHTS[11]

The "Universal Declaration of Human Rights (UDHR)" is a landmark manuscript in the history of human rights. It was drafted by various signatories and legislative bodies representing different cultural backgrounds and legal backgrounds from every corner of the world. On 10th December 1948 "(General Assembly resolution 217 A)" in Paris the "United Nations General Assembly" proclaimed and declared the "Universal Declaration of Human Rights (UDHR)" as the general standard of attainment for every citizen and for all the nations. This was the first attempt to ensure that fundamental human rights should be universally safeguarded. It consists of 30 articles and more than 500 languages have been translated so far.

Preamble

The acceptance of the inborn dignity, equality, and undeniable rights of all individuals is the basis of justice, peace, and freedom in the world without discrimination.

In contrast, disrespect and accusations of human rights violation lead to ferocious acts, which have heated the sense of right and wrong, and the beginning of the world in which mankind shall benefit from the liberty of speech, liberty from fear, and belief has been publicly announced as the utmost ambition of the general people.

In contrast, it is necessary that if an individual does not have an alternative as a way out, to revolt against cruelty and repression. The rule of law should make sure that human rights are protected,

---

[11] Universal Declaration of Human Rights

In contrast, it is necessary to endorse the expansion of friendship and good relations among the nations.

In contrast, in the agreement, the United Nations have strongly confirmed their faith in fundamental human rights, the value of human lives, identical rights of women and men, and has resolved to encourage social advancement and enhanced standards of human life with liberty.

In contrast, the Member States have taken an oath to accomplish, in collaboration with the United Nations, the endorsement of universal respect for and observation of human rights and fundamental freedoms.

In contrast, a general understanding of these rights and liberty is of greater importance for the complete recognition of this pledge.

Now, Therefore, "THE GENERAL ASSEMBLY" proclaims "THIS UNIVERSAL DECLARATION OF HUMAN RIGHTS" as a general

standard of attainment for all humankind and all the nations, till the end that every person and every organ of society, keeping this announcement continuously in mind, shall endeavor by teaching and education to endorse admiration for these rights and liberty and by progressive procedures, national and international, to protect their universal and effective identification and observation, both among the peoples of Member States themselves and among the peoples of territories under their jurisdiction.

Articles 1 to 30 comprised of all the rights and freedoms entitled to mankind and its contents have been summarized accordingly.

- Every person is born free and equal in dignity and rights.
- Every person should show the spirit of brotherhood.
- Everyone is entitled to all the rights and freedoms set forth in this Declaration, without distinction of any kind, such as race, color, sex, language, religion, political or other opinion, national or social origin, property, birth or other social status.
- There should not be any distinction based on jurisdiction, political parties, international territory, and status of the country.
- Everybody can enjoy the right to liberty, life, and security.

- Nobody should be kept in bondage or slavery. The Slave trade and slavery are strictly prohibited in all their forms.
- Prohibition of torture, cruelty, inhuman treatment, or punishment to any individual.
- Everybody has the right to recognition everywhere as a person before the law.
- Everyone is equal before the law and is equally protected by the law without any discrimination.
- Everybody has the right to an effective remedy by the competent national tribunals for acts violating the fundamental rights granted by the constitution or by law.
- Prohibition of exile, detention, or arbitrary arrest.
- Everybody is entitled in full equality to a fair and public hearing in the court for any criminal accusation against him.
- Anybody charged with a severe offense has the right to be presumed innocent until proven guilty and no other heavier penalty shall be enforced apart from the penalty which was imposed at the time of the severe offense committed.
- Nobody should be subjected to arbitrary interference with his privacy, family, home or correspondence, or to attacks upon his honour and reputation. Everybody has the right to be protected against such interference or attack.
- Everybody has the freedom and right to move freely and reside anywhere within their own country.
- Everybody has the right to leave any country, including their own country, and to return to their country.
- Everybody has the right to escape from persecution by taking asylum in another country.
- Nobody can deny the right of a person's nationality.
- The nationality of a person should not be deprived arbitrarily. Nobody can be denied the right to change their nationality.

- Marriage should not be limited due to religion or nationality and it has to be taken with the full approval of the two spouses.
- Family is considered as the natural and primary component of society and it has to be protected by society and the State.
- Everybody has the right to own any property individually or in partnership with others.
- A person should not be deprived of their property arbitrarily.
- Everybody has the freedom and right to change his belief or religion, either with the community or alone and in private or public.
- Everybody has the freedom and right to share and express opinions, which includes receiving ideas and imparting information through media despite the frontiers.
- Everybody has the freedom and right to hold a peaceful assembly or association and nobody should be forced to become a member of an association.
- Everybody has the right to take part in government and have free access to public services in his country.
- Everybody is a member of society and has the right to cultural and social security.
- Everybody has the right to work without discrimination, with equal pay for equal work, freedom of choice for employment, to work in favorable conditions, and to form or join any trade union.
- Everybody has the right to leisure and rest, including reasonable limitation of working hours and periodic paid holidays.
- Everybody has the right to a standard of living adequate for the health and well-being of himself and his family, including clothing, food, medical care, housing, and essential social services, and the right to security in the event of unemployment, disability, sickness, old age, widowhood, or other circumstances beyond his control.
- Children born within and outside of marriage should be given equal social care and protection.

- Everyone has the right to education. Education shall be free, at least in the elementary and fundamental stages. Elementary education shall be compulsory. Parents also have the initial right to decide the type of education to be given to their children. Professional and Technical education shall be made generally available and higher education shall be equally accessible to everyone based on merit.

- Education shall be emphasized fully for the development of human personality and to strengthen respect for human rights to promote tolerance, understanding, and friendship between nations.

- Everybody has the right to freely participate in the cultural life of their community. Everybody has the right to protect the moral, literary, artistic, and scientific production of his authorship.

- Article 28, "Everyone is entitled to a social and international order in which the rights and freedoms outlined in this Declaration can be fully realized."

- Article 29 (3), "These rights and freedoms may in no case be exercised contrary to the purposes and principles of the United Nations."

- Article 30, "Nothing in this Declaration may be interpreted as implying for any State, group or person any right to engage in any activity or to perform any act aimed at the destruction of any of the rights and freedoms set forth herein."

3

NATIONAL HUMAN RIGHTS COMMISSION

NHRC Establishment in India and its Functions[12]

On 12th October 1993, The National Human Rights Commission (NHRC) was formed. Its decree is enclosed in the "Protection of Human Rights Act, 1993," and complies with the "Paris Principles" embraced at the "first international workshop on national institutions" for the endorsement and safeguard of "human rights" held in 1991 at Paris during October and authorized by the "General Assembly of the United Nations in Resolution 48/134 on 20th December 1993." The National Human Rights Commission (NHRC) is a tangible form of India's apprehension for the encouragement and safeguarding of "Human rights."

Distinctive Features of NHRC

Under the National Human Rights Commission, some distinctive features are different from other Commissions/ autonomous institutions/regulatory bodies.

- NHRC is a self-governing body created by an Act of Parliament
- NHRC is devoted to providing self-determining views on matters inside the vernacular of the Constitution or in law for the constant safeguard of human rights. The NHRC operates independently and should not be arbitrarily deprived.
- NHRC The NHRC has full control of a civil court when trying a suit under the 'Code of Civil Procedure, 1908' concerning summons. It can enforce the presence of witnesses, receive confirmation on affidavits, discover and produce any files, claim any public copy or record from the office or court, provide payment for the assessment of evidence or documents, and appeal public records, as mentioned in 'Section 13 of the Act.
- NHRC gives the power to donate provisional aid.
- NHRC gives the power to suggest and pay for damages or reimbursement.
- Around 70000 complaints are made each year, which shows the reliability of the Commission and the increase in hopes of the general public.

---

[12] The National Human Rights Commission India

- NHRC has broad consent.
- NHRC has distinctive machinery which examines the execution of several suggestions.

Functions

The Commission has a broad directive that includes "civil and political rights, social, economic and cultural rights, and group rights." In Section XII, it is stated that NHRC will carry out these functions:

- Suo Motu, on questioning or on petitions, offered to it by the sufferers, or any other individual on behalf of them, or verdict of any magistrate, on a direction, into the grievance of human rights offense or instigating a person to commit an offense thereof carelessness in the avoidance of such offense, by a public servant.
- Interceding in all forms of schedule that involve any accusation of human rights offense that are still waiting before the Court, with the permission of the Courts.
- Visits, despite obstacles, enforced for the time being in other laws, other institutions, or jails under the command of the State Government, in which individuals are lodged and detained purposely for action, protection, reformation, or to study the living situation of the jailers and making suitable suggestions.
- Making a review of the safeguards provided by the Constitution, underneath, or any other law enforced for the time being to protect human rights, and suggesting actions for successful execution.
- Reviewing issues, including terrorist acts, which restrain people from enjoying human rights, and propose suitable corrective action.
- Studying various protocols and international instruments on human rights, to suggest suitable advice for successful execution.
- Taking up research and promoting human rights research.
- Educating human rights knowledge in several sections of the society, and creating awareness about the protection accessible for safeguarding human rights by publishing books, holding conferences, seminars, and through media and other accessible sources.
- Encouraging the hard work of NGOs and other institutions that provide services for human rights.
- Undertaking all the functions which are identified to be essential for promoting human rights.

4

UNIVERSAL DECLARATION OF HUMAN RIGHTS AND INDIAN CONSTITUTION

Under the Indian constitution, human rights do not exist in a vacuum. Inevitably, they are more or less formulated by the central government and implemented by the state itself. India itself is a signatory to the Universal Declaration of Human Rights (UDHR) and does not deny the value of Human rights. However, many state, regional, national, and international bodies are taking responsibility to oversee and monitor human rights and ensure their implementation by the state.

On November 26, 1949, after having long discussions and debates in the constituent Assembly, the constitution of India came into force. The framing of the constitution of India was through the impact of the idea of human rights and assured most of the human rights contained in the UDHR. The UDHR includes Political and Civil rights as well as Cultural, Economic, and Social rights. "Part III of Indian Constitution" i.e. "Fundamental rights incorporated Civil and Political Rights" and "Part IV of Indian Constitution" i.e. "Directive Principles of State Policy incorporated Economic, Social, and Cultural rights." The conclusive enclosure of the significant provisions of UDHR has given supremacy above all the constitutional provisions in India.

Table no. 1.1 shows the similarities between "Civil and Political Rights of UDHR" and "Part III of Indian Constitution" i.e. Fundamental rights. Almost all the important rights and provisions of UDHR Civil and Political rights are incorporated in Part III Fundamental Rights of the Indian Constitution.

Table no. 1.1

Civil and Political Rights in the Fundamental Rights of the Indian Constitution and the Universal Declaration of Human Rights.

Sl. No	Indian Constitution Part III (Fundamental rights)	Universal Declaration
1	Article 21 The Right to Life and Personal Liberty.	Article 3, Everybody has the right to life, liberty, and security.
2	Article 23 Prohibition of trafficking of human beings and forced labor.	Article 4, Nobody shall be held in slavery or servitude; slavery and slave trade shall be prohibited in any form.
3	Articles 14 and 15 Equality before the law and no discrimination against any citizen on grounds of religion, race, caste, sex, or place of birth.	Article 7, Equality before the law and Non- discrimination.
4	Article 32 Granted the Supreme Court and the High Courts, the power to issue writs to protect the fundamental rights of the citizens.	Article 8, Right to an effective remedy.
5	Article 22 Protection against arrest and detention in certain cases.	Article 9, Rights against arbitrary arrest, detention, and right to habeas corpus.

6	Article 20 (1) No person shall be convicted of any offence except for violation of the law in force at the time of the commission of the act charged as an offence, or be subjected to a penalty greater than that as commission.	Article 11, Rights to Ex-post facto law.
7	Article 19 (1) (d) right to move freely throughout the territory of India.	Article 13 (1), Right to freedom of movement.
8	Article 19 (1) (f) Right to acquire, hold, and dispose of the property. (Omitted by the 42nd Amendment).	Article 17, Right to own property and not be deprived of property.
9	Article 25 (1) Freedom of conscience and the right to freely profess, practice, and propagate religion.	Article 18, Right to freedom of thought, conscience, and religion.
10	Article 19 (1) (a) Right to freedom of speech and expression.	Article 19, Right to freedom of opinion and expression.
11	Article 19 (1) (b) Right to assemble peacefully and without arms.	Article 20 (1), Right to freedom of peaceful assembly and association.
12	Article 16 (1) Equality of opportunity for all citizens in matters relating to employment or appointment to any office under the State.	Article 21 (1), Right to equal access to public service.
13	Article 29 (1) Any section of the citizens having a distinct language or culture has the right to conserve.	Article 22, Right to social security.
14	Article 19 (1) (c) Freedom of Association or Union.	Article 23, Right to form or join a trade union.

17

5
MANIPUR HUMAN RIGHTS COMMISSION

Manipur Human Rights Commission (MHRC) is often referred to as the "Sign Board" Commission of Manipur. This observation was made by the former Chairperson of MHRC, Justice Late W.A. Shishak, (former Chief Justice of the High Court of Chhattisgarh and Himachal Pradesh) when asked about the status of the Commission.

Every state in our country was mandated to have an act on human rights as per the goals of the structural program undertaken by India during the period of liberalization. As a result, an act popularly known as the Protection of Human Rights Act was formed in 1993; consequently, it was amended in 2006. This Act is the backbone for creating Human Rights Commissions in every state, including the Manipur Human Rights Commission (MHRC). Concerning the Protection of Human Rights Act 1993, the Manipur Human Rights Commission (MHRC) was formed on 27th June 1998. Justice Surendra Nath Bhargava, retired Chief Justice of the Sikkim High Court, was appointed as the first Chairperson; he was also the Chairperson of the Assam Human Rights Commission. The members were appointed on 13th October 1998 and took their responsibility with effect from 10th December 1998.

Unfortunately, since 2010, the Manipur State Commission has been defunct after the retirement of Chairman Chief Justice W.A. Shishak and Colonel R.K Rajendra, N.G Nongyai, and M Gourachand. The dysfunction of the State Human Rights Commission has been discussed by various concerned civil organizations and an appeal has been made tentatively to the State government. The reformation of the Commission occurs once the Chairperson and all the members complete their tenure. However, due to dysfunctional systems in the State, grievances and petitions cannot be filed at the commission. As a result, the office of the State Human Rights

Commission remains closed for extended periods. This prolonged closure has led to a lack of justice delivery, raising concerns about government inefficiency. A few years ago, the present Chief Minister, N. Biren Singh, initiated efforts to revive the commission, although its activities are primarily concentrated in the valley areas.

Main purpose and functions

The power and functions of the Manipur Human Rights Commission are more fully prescribed and mentioned in "Section 12 of the Protection of Human Rights Act, 1993"; they are as follows:

(a) Make inquiries, suo-motu or on a petition given by the victim or any individual on behalf of the victim, complaining of:

(i) Human rights violations or

(ii) Carelessness and failure to prevent such violation by the public servant.

(b) Intervene in all forms of proceedings that involve any accusation of human rights offense that are still waiting before the Court with the permission of the Court.

(c) Visit any state government prison or other institution with the concerned State Government, in which individuals are kept and detained purposely for action, protection, or reformation, to study the living situation of the inmates and make suitable suggestions.

(d) Make a review of the safeguards provided by the Constitution or underneath or any other law implemented temporarily to safeguard human rights and suggest actions for successful implementation.

(e) Understanding the matters, which include terrorist acts that prevent the privilege of human rights and providing necessary suggestions and corrective measures.

(f) Examining international agreements and other approaches to human rights and proposing suggestions for their successful implementation.

(g) Undertaking responsibility and promoting human rights research.

(h) Spreading human rights education in various groups of society by promoting precaution and for the protection and safeguarding of human rights through publications of books and journals, media, conferences, seminars, and various other sources.

(i) Encouraging the hard work of NGOs and other institutions working for human rights.

(j) And other functions that are recognized as essential elements for human rights promotion.

As contemplated in Sub-section (a). (ii) of "Section 12 of the Protection of Human Rights Act, 1993", the Manipur Human Rights Commission inquires, suo motu, or on a petition submitted to it by the sufferer or any individual on behalf of him. In the event of filing a complaint contemplated in Sub-section (a). (ii) of "Section 12 of the Protection of Human Rights Act, 1993" by a victim complaining about a human rights violation or forcing someone to commit a crime or carelessness shown in preventing violation of human rights by a public servant, the Commission has to inquire into the complaint by following the procedures prescribed in Section 17 of the Act of 1993.

6

CONSTITUTIONAL RIGHTS FOR TRIBALS[13]

In India, tribals constitute 8.6 % of the total population, presenting a population of 104.3 million as per the 2011 census and they are the most neglected community in availing rights and justice due to ignorance. The Tribal communities are known to be the most marginalized group in India because of their disadvantages and exploitation by outsiders. Tribal communities enjoy fewer opportunities and are deprived of their inherent rights in every social aspect. As compared to the rest of the mainland, they have more burdens and have been going through bitter sufferings since time immemorial.

There are 33 recognized ST communities in Manipur, which constitute 34.41% of the state population as per the 2011 census. Even though the constitution of India gives several rights and protection to the tribal population, the tribals of Manipur remain backward, and their rights are being neglected in many ways. The tribals are the most backward as compared to the general population and also compared with the other backward groups like Scheduled castes, which are also under the same constitutional protection for their upliftment.

Article 366 (25) of the Indian constitution alludes to scheduled tribes, considering those communities as scheduled tribes with reference to Article 342 of the Indian Constitution. As per Article 342 of the Indian Constitution, the Scheduled tribes are considered as those tribes or the tribal communities or part of or within the groups of these tribes and tribal communities which the President declared through public announcement. Article 14 of the Indian Constitution states:

---

[13] Government of India, "National Commission for Schedule tribes"

The state shall not reject any individual's equality as per the law or the equal safeguards of the laws inside the territory of India. In India, the tribals are considered weaker and relatively inferior to other communities, which often leads to them being looked down on and treated differently. However, the Constitution of India provides several rights to protect the tribals from any kind of exploitation and assures to safeguard their interests and inherent rights.

I. Cultural and Educational protection

Article 15 (4) provides special provisions to the other backward classes including Scheduled tribes for their development.

Article 29 gives protection to the Interests of Minorities including Scheduled Tribes.

Article 46 gives the provision for the State to promote, with special care, to uplift educational standards and economic well-being of the weaker sections, particularly for the Scheduled Tribes and Scheduled Castes, and to safeguard the weaker sections from all forms of exploitation and social injustice.

Article 350 gives the right to preserve the distinct Culture, Script, and Language.

Article 350 gives the choice of instruction through the mother tongue.

II. Social protection

Article 23 prohibits the trafficking of human beings and all forms of forced labor.

Article 24 Forbids Child Labor.

III. Economic protection

Article 244 Clause (1) provides provisions of the Fifth Schedule which shall be applied to the administration and control of the Scheduled Tribes in any state except in the states of Meghalaya, Assam, Tripura, and Mizoram.

Article 275 provides Grants-in-Aid to specified Scheduled tribe States.

IV. Political protection

Article 164 (1) Provision of Tribal Affairs Ministers in Orissa, Bihar, and Madhya Pradesh.

Article 330 provides reservation of seats in Lok Sabha for the Scheduled tribes.

Article 337 provides reservation of seats in State Legislatures for the Scheduled tribes.

Article 334 provides reservation for a period of 10 years.

Article 243 provides reservation of seats for Scheduled tribes in Panchayats.

Article 371 provides special provisions for the Northeast States and Sikkim.

V. Service protection

Articles 16 (4), 16 (4A), 164 (B) **Article** 335, and **Article** 320 (40) provide services and safeguards for the Scheduled tribes.

Safeguards under various Laws for STs

(1) The Scheduled Tribes and Scheduled Castes (Prevention of Atrocities) Act, 1989.

(2) Bonded Labor System (Abolition) Act 1976 (for Scheduled Tribes).

(3) Child Labor (Prohibition and Regulation) Act 1986.

(4) States Acts & Regulations concerning alienation and restoration of land belonging to Scheduled tribes.

(5) Forest Conservation Act 1980 for Scheduled tribes.

(6) Panchayati Raj (Extension to Scheduled Areas) Act 1996.

(7) Minimum Wages Act of 1948.

(8) The Scheduled Tribes and Scheduled Castes (Prevention of Atrocities) Amendment Act, 2015.

7

ARMED FORCES SPECIAL POWER ACT (AFSPA) 1958

Power given to Armed Forces under the AFSP Act 1958[14]

The Armed Forces (Special Powers) Ordinance was promulgated by the British on August 15, 1942, to suppress the Quit India Movement. The ordinance later evolved into an Act that grants special powers to the armed forces personnel in designated "disturbed areas" of the Northeastern States, including Assam, Arunachal Pradesh, Manipur, Tripura, Meghalaya, Mizoram, and Nagaland.

The Act guarantees the following special powers to any military officer, warrant officer, commissioned officer, non-commissioned officer, and any other person of equivalent rank in the military forces, air forces operating as land forces, and other operating armed forces of the Union.

Provisions included in the AFSPA as enacted by the Parliament in the Ninth Year of the Republic of India are as follows:

- Power to declare areas to be disturbed areas.
- Special powers of the armed forces.
- Power to hand arrested people over to the police.
- Army officers have legal immunity for their actions.

Armed Forces Special Power Act 1958 is an ongoing debate and is contrary to fundamental rights. The Indian Armed Forces and State Commandos have misused their power on the pretext of AFSPA; there is no guarantee for safety and social security. However, taking one's life seems to be an

---

[14] The Armed Forces (Special Powers) Act, 1958 Act No. 28 of 1958, 11th September, 1958

authorized prerogative for the Armed Forces. The Tangkhul community has participated in several protests and peace rallies to repeal the Act from Ukhrul but to no avail.

Rules under Section 144 of the Criminal Procedure Code

According to this Section, a Magistrate can prohibit the assembly of more than five people in an area in any part of the country. According to sections 141-149 of the Indian Penal Code (IPC), severe imprisonment for three years or a fine is imposed as a punishment for those who engage in rioting. Any member organizing an unlawful assembly of more than five people will be held responsible for any crime committed by the members with or without any consent.

Section 144 of CrPC is applied as per the opinion of the magistrate when "there is sufficient ground for proceeding under this section." Under this section, it prohibits provoking danger to human life, health, and safety. This prohibition is recommended to prevent "disturbance of the public tranquility." Such prohibition indicates that too much raising of voice will end in Lathi Charge by the Armed forces.[15]

Historical Background of AFSPA in Manipur

AFSPA was implemented in the Naga Hills and some areas of the then Assam state. Over time, it has extended to other Northeastern states of India. In opposition to this Act, the Naga National Council protested and boycotted the first general election of India in 1952, which was later extended to boycotting government colleges, government schools, and all government offices. The situation worsened and the Assam Disturbed Areas Act of 1955 was enacted, leading to the deployment of Assam Rifles in the Naga-inhabited hill areas with the intention to demolish Naga rebels. The paramilitary forces and the armed state police force could not contain the Naga insurgents as the Naga movement became fiercer and later the Naga insurgents and the Naga Nationalist Council (NNC) initiated a corresponding government "The Federal Government of Nagaland" on 23rd March 1956. Later, the "Armed Forces Special Powers Ordinance" was propagated by the then President Dr. Rajendra Prasad on 22nd May 1958, but it was replaced by the "Armed Forces (Assam and Manipur) Special Powers Act, 1958" on 11th September 1958.

---

[15] Know your laws: "CrPC, Section 144, 'Prohibition of Assembly'."

The "Armed Forces (Assam and Manipur) Special Powers Act" was signed into law in the Parliament of India, which gives special powers to the Armed Forces in "disturbed areas". Once the state is termed a disturbed area, the state has to maintain a minimum of three months of status quo. The Central Govt., the Heads of State, and the Union Territories have the authority to declare the states or the regions as "disturbed areas." This act grants extraordinary powers to the Armed Forces as well as immunity from any legal action, and the right to shoot, kill, or arrest suspects without giving any warrants.

The revolt against the Naga movement and other counterpart insurgents' activities became a serious and urgent issue in the state, resulting in the declaration of "Disturbed Areas" on 11th September 1980, followed by enforcement of Section 144 of the Criminal Procedure Code (S.144 CrPC) on 13th July 2014 has brought adverse effect in regards to peace and harmony of the state. The Union Home Minister on 24th March 2023, announced the removal of the Act from the jurisdiction of 19 police stations from the six valley districts. The six valley districts are Imphal West, Imphal East, Thoubal, Bishnupur, Kakching, and Jiribam. The order, effective from April 1, would be applicable for six months whereas, the hill districts remain untouched. Due to the imposition of AFSPA the hill districts have been deprived of their rights and their cry for justice is unheeded. Chief Minister N. Biren had stated that his government is urging the Prime Minister to materialize the issue as per the desire of the people of the State and the people of the Northeast.[16]

Problems of AFSPA in Manipur

India is the largest democratic country, yet the value of human rights has been immensely disparaged and the constitution seems to be vague for many of the citizens of the state. The Armed Forces have demeaned the dignity of the citizens and are directly and indirectly ruled by the ruthless AFSPA. Due to the Armed Forces (Special Powers) Act (AFSPA), several human rights have been violated to a large extent, including condoning extrajudicial killings in the state. Even though they are accountable for the violations and crimes committed, they are safeguarded by the Constitution. This has created a new category of Indian citizens who are considered 'killable' people and 'rape-able' women, says

---

[16] https://newsonair.gov.in/News?title=Manipur%3a-CM-N.-Biren-Singh-expresses-gratitude-to-PM-Modi-for-trying-to-revoke-AFSPA-from-Northeast-region&id=440068

Babloo Loitongbam, a human rights activist and lawyer. In the space of 33 years, a concrete record of at least 1,528 extrajudicial executions of civilians has been documented. In protest to repeal this draconian law, Irom Sharmila, the Iron Lady of Manipur, continued hunger strikes for 16 long years but was unsuccessful in abrogating it.

The Armed Forces Special Powers Act (AFSPA) has committed numerous gross human rights violations, even though it is backed by the Constitution. The public opinion and perception of AFSPA have not changed in Manipur; it has always been seen as anti-people, giving the Armed Forces license to act with impunity, violating human rights without liability. AFSPA gives the Armed Forces personnel the power to arrest suspects without a warrant and shoot or kill the suspects, making it clear that the Act is in violation of human rights law. The unforgettable incident and the misuse of power and unconstitutional amendment by the Armed Forces is still unforgivable to this day by the people of Manipur.

AFSPA is all about providing protection to the Armed Forces and is indirectly encouraging them to commit human rights violations. When a state is declared a disturbed area by the central government, AFSPA is enforced in order to bring normal functioning to the broken government. The motives and objectives of imposing AFSPA are to restore normalcy by deploying the Armed Forces. However, its indefinite deployment has unfortunately resulted in the violation of human rights and loaded strife in the community. In a democratic country, human rights have to be respected and even any Act or deployment of the Armed Forces should be for a limited period.

The central and the state government have failed to protect and provide security to the people of Manipur. While the poor governance and insurgency problem may be the ultimate reason for the imposition of AFSPA, there is an underlying agenda that the local population is not aware of. There is no denying that strict provisions of law, including this Act, are necessary and perfectly valid in areas with the presence of militancy or insurgency. However, in a democratic country, public opinion and perception should be respected. This cannot be taken for granted and public opinion must be examined and reviewed to determine whether the Act is making sense to the local community or not. If it is becoming a threat to the local community, it is much wiser to repeal and withdraw the Act without any condition, for the benefit of the citizens.

With concern on humanitarian grounds, the government took a massive step to create awareness, and a better understanding of the sentiments of the public, which resulted in setting up a commission under the leadership of one retd. Judge of the Supreme Court for assessing the Act, the "Jeevan Reddy Commission," in which a retd. general of the Indian army is one of the members, who collectively suggested the repeal of AFSPA and to be replaced with a suitable amendment. AFSPA has been a burning issue in the Northeastern states and Jammu and Kashmir in general. Hence, the central government is trying to bring changes anyhow. So far, no final decision on the recommendation has been made because the Armed Forces have made delays in repealing the Act and bringing any changes to the Act. Yet the government of India has given assurance to repeal the Act but has failed to do so, to date. This issue was discussed at Imphal more than six years back but it has not yet been solved even after many years.

Regrettably, the situation of the Ukhrul district is quite peculiar and contradicts the constitutional rights established for the protection of citizens. The district was labeled as a 'disturbed area' even before the imposition of AFSPA in the state on 8th September 1980, primarily due to the presence of the Naga Movement. The reality is that, even in times of peace and harmony in the state, it is consistently labeled as disturbed due to ongoing hostilities. This, in turn, allows the Armed Forces to exploit AFSPA, leading to egregious violations of human rights. The Armed forces' "own mechanisms" are enough to claim their rights and the Armed forces become undisputed in several human rights violation cases. In the process, numerous cases arose where the armed forces became unapproachable to the victims. The lack of concrete and fair judgments within the court-martial legal process has shielded culprits with impunity. Despite several protests and rallies being staged, both at the Central and State levels, they went unnoticed by the government, resulting in much of the agitation and protests going in vain.

The citizenship of Luingam Luithui, a human rights activist from the district, was illegally revoked for 22 years by the Ministry of Home Affairs (MHA). He and his wife Peingamla were forced to become refugees and live in exile in Canada and seek the protection of the United Nations High Commissioner for Refugees (UNHCR). However, Luingam Luithui fought back and the Delhi High Court finally restored the Indian citizenship of both Luingam Luithui and his wife on 24th August 2017.[17] It is observed that those who are against the rules and regulations of the government are often punished and considered a threat to national integrity. Hence, many sensible citizens who stood for Naga's cause were victimized and punished unprecedentedly.

The entire Ukhrul district, along with Tangkhul villages in other districts, has faced severe consequences due to the imposition of Section 144 of the Criminal Procedure Code (CrPC) and the Armed Forces (Special Powers) Act (AFSPA). The Tangkhul community has endured numerous instances of egregious human rights violations perpetrated by both the Central Armed Forces and State Armed Forces. The implementation of AFSPA has given rise to numerous allegations of human rights violations, contributing to a range of social issues and unrest within the Tangkhul community.

---

[17] Indian citizenship regained: "The 22-year ordeal of Luingam Luithui for justice," Edited by *Joyjeet Das*

8
NATURE OF HUMAN RIGHTS VIOLATION

Ever since the imposition of the AFSPA 1958 in Ukhrul in 1958, the Tangkhul community has been subjected to victimization by the Armed Forces and has been struggling for a peaceful existence. The maximum cases of human rights violations are recorded from four blocks in seven villages: Ukhrul headquarters, Huining village, Talui village, Ngainga village, Kumrum village, Jessami village, and Huishu village. Every household in these villages has suffered from various forms of gross human rights violations. The increasing activity of terrorism in the district has exacerbated social tension, and the imposition of the AFSP Act 1958 has further ignited enmity between the community and the Indian Armed Forces. Knowing that the State and the Central government have continuously failed to solve human rights issues, the community has lost its hopes and expectations to recuperate its rights. For more than decades, the Armed Forces have committed numerous gross human rights violations in various forms.

The Nature of Human Rights Violations:

- Physical torture and harassment.
- Corporal punishment.
- Labor work as punishment.
- Human shield from bullets.
- Forced porter.
- Ragging and threatening.
- Outraging modesty while torturing.
- Killing innocent people on suspicion of firing.

- Fake encounter.
- Extrajudicial killing.
- Arrest without warrant.
- Rape and molestation of women.
- Sodomy.
- Restriction of movement at night.
- Detention on suspicion.
- Kidnap.
- Mental harassment.
- Grouping of villagers.
- House raid.
- Robbery.
- Checking on commuters.
- Fleeing of youth from the village.
- Arson attack on villages.
- Enforced disappearance.
- Imposing fines on the pretext of supporting insurgents.
- Extortion.
- Damaging properties.
- Trigger and escalate violence.
- Electric shock.
- Body check on commuters.
- Raining tear gas, smoke bombs, and live bullets.
- Illegal occupation of villages

9

NAGA PEOPLE'S MOVEMENT FOR HUMAN RIGHTS (NPMHR)[18]

The Naga People's Movement for Human Rights (NPMHR) was formed on September 9, 1978, as a response to the needs of the long struggle of the Naga people to organize this movement and to promote human rights, which have been suppressed under militant rule for decades. NPMHR aims to initiate a movement for the Naga people and be their voice to encourage them to fight for their rights by disclosing their side of the story to mainland India and also to the rest of the world while also fighting against the imperialist policy of the central government and such draconian acts like AFSPA. Nagas have a unique history and have been intensely maintaining their political rights and cultural autonomy since time immemorial. Therefore, NPMHR strives to deal with the various human rights violation issues and advocate for the rights of the Naga people.

Declaration of NPMHR

The history of Nagas has come out from a great struggle, fighting for freedom from suppression, domination, and exploitation. No history ever remains great without the struggle for existence and independence. Naga history has shown the existence of forces exerted by different machinery directly or indirectly that affect the Naga social system. For decades, Nagas have been experiencing socio-economic exploitation, political suppression, and domination by Armed forces under the enforcement of AFSPA in Naga-inhabited areas.

Thus, the 'Naga People's Movement for Human Rights' took up the responsibility to initiate an organized movement to achieve the following:

---

[18] Naga People's Movement for Human Rights documents.

To guarantee and protect:

1. Right to life.
2. Right to work.
3. Right to live collectively and merger of the Naga Lands.
4. Right to uphold and share one's ideas.
5. Freedom of assembly, association, and movement
6. Liberty to access public places.
7. Full involvement of all the members in decision-making to bring an effect on their lives.
8. Liberty from all forms of exploitation, political control, and military suppression.
9. Liberty from the undemocratic system and the demolition of institutions and social ethics that validate and preserve the society.
10. Liberty from the system of random arrest, confinement, torment, execution, and use of unlawful machinery.
11. Liberty from the enforcement of disagreeable external legal systems, socio-cultural ideas, and conduct of life.

NPMHR does not deal with the violation of human rights only, but it is concerned with the state structure and the development model maintaining ecological balance and violence. The various Programs of NPMHR include awareness programs, promotions, and protection of Human Rights, publicizing and documenting Human Rights Violations which includes forwarding cases to the Supreme/High Courts of India against such human rights violations; organising relief work for the human rights violations victims through economic programs of rehabilitation and so forth. All these are also important aspects of NPMHR.

10

TANGKHUL NAGA

History of Tangkhul Naga Tribe

According to T.C. Hodson, the origin of the Tangkhul Naga tribe was first recorded at Hunpung, it is believed that Hunpung is the center of the dispersion of the Tangkhul Naga tribe. The word "Nagas" and its meaning is still a matter of debate as the exact derivation is still not known to date. According to A.D. Ptolemy, a famous Greek Geographer of Egypt, in the 2nd Century, remarks "Nangalogae" to a group of people. In Sanskrit, the word, "Nangalogae" (Nanga Log) is known as "Naked" People. According to John Butler, It was the people of the plains who used to call them Naga because they were found naked. W.C. Smith is of the view that the root word of Naga is 'Noga', which itself has been derived from the word 'Nok', which means people. It was the term 'Nok', which in due course of time became Naga. Sir Gait also agrees with the same view and regards the word 'Nok' as the root of the term Naga. Elwin finds the origin of the term Naga in the local tongue as 'Nok', which means people, and that is similar to Tibeto-Burman languages.[19] According to Burmese tradition, the term "NAGA" is said to have its roots in the word "NAKA," where 'NA' represents ear and 'GA' is associated with hole, meaning "people with perforated ears". As per the Burmese observation during the migratory period, it was seen that Nagas pierced their earlobe and inserted a big wooden piece or other attractive ornaments as they passed through the Burmese region. This view, in fact, appears convincing and realistic.

As per the foretold story, the Tangkhul Naga tribe is said to have migrated from Maikhel Tunggam village, comprising the common aboriginal inhabitants of the Quassi - Angami and Mao groups. According to T.C. Hudson in 1220 A.D.

---

[19] The Naga Society, Dr. Chandra Singh (2008) Manas Publication.

when the Shan invaded Assam, the Nagas were resisting their invasion (T.C. Hudson "The Naga tribes of Manipur London" 1911). Despite everything, Nagas accept that they are a Mongoloid race; it is also agreed that originally, the Tangkhul Nagas belonged to Mongoloid race. When tracing the history of the Tangkhul Nagas, it is believed that from 10,000 B.C. to 8000 B.C., they inhabited an area beside the Huang Heo and Yangtze Rivers (in the Xinjiang province of China). The Tangkhul Nagas, including other people, migrated in diverse directions due to poor sources of livelihood. Some of them moved towards the eastern direction and southeast and later merged with the Chinese people while other groups moved towards the southward direction and became the tribe of Tibeto-Burman, including the Tangkhul Naga and other Naga tribes.

Tangkhul

The term "Tangkhul" is a mystery and debatable for many scholars since there is no written document or concrete narration about its origins. Though the Tangkhul term may be confusing, there are some theories and assumptions that open up their opinion as per their findings and evidence.

According to Stephen Angkang, Tangkhul is a word coined very recently by the Britishers Pemberton through a Meitei interpreter Lairenjao, it is derived from two words 'Atongba' which means elevated place and 'Khul' which means village because the Tangkhul settled in elevated places (hills). It was recorded as 'Tongkhul' but over time, it was changed into Tangkhul.

Other differing opinions suggest Tangkhul is a terminology of two Meitei words, Tada (Brother) and Khun (Village). Another version of the origin of the term tangkhul is that it is derived from two Meitei words, Atāngbā Khun. The word 'Atāngbā' means scarcity or poor on the one hand, and rare or unique on the other hand, and 'Khun' means village. It is also believed that the word Tangkhul comes from Than-Khul, a combination of the Burmese word 'Than' (iron) and Meitei 'Khul' (village).

Another version of the origin of the term Tangkhul came from the local dialect, "Tangpat kahai akhur" meaning "neat and smooth hole or cave". As per the oral folklore within the Nagas, it is told that the Tangkhuls, along with some Naga tribes, came out from the cave of Makhel, which is in Senapati district, Manipur. It is also said that the hole of the cave became very smooth due to the continuous movement of the people. But regardless of all these propounded theories, it is normally accepted and assumed that the name of this tribe is derived from the Meities, who are the nearest neighbors to Tangkhul.

The Tangkhul community primarily inhabits Kamjong and Ukhrul districts of Manipur. Ukhrul, an area consisting of Hunphun and Hunpung villages, is the headquarters of the Tangkhul community. Tangkhul community is unique, and they are known for their rich culture. Other tribes are highly fascinated by their traditional attires and ornaments. Tangkhuls are also lovers of songs and music. Their folk songs and folk dances are very popular; they play traditional musical instruments like Tingteila (traditional Violin), Pung (traditional Drum), and Sipa (traditional Flute) to harmonize their folk songs. In addition to its uniqueness, every Tangkhul village has its own local dialect. Hunphun dialect is spoken as a common language among all the Tangkhul; a slightly modified English alphabet is used as a script, which was taught by the American Baptist Missionary William Pettigrew.

Traditionally, the Tangkhul tribe used to settle in different hilly areas for safety and security, as they are independent and self-reliant on their local land and forests. Their governance is a democratic system, constituted by the Village Chief (Awunga) and the Village Council (Hanga). They have a strong political system that has existed since their inception. Tangkhul's forefathers believed in Zingwunga/ Reisāngchonme, who is considered the almighty.

Normally, Meitei term Tangkhuls as 'Hao/Hau', which is a sign of affronting or insulting the hill people (Ching-mi) with the advent of Hinduism in the valley; alleging that the hill people as 'inferior' and they as 'superior' one. Many Tangkhuls believe the term 'Hao' is the original nomenclature of the Tangkhuls.

Tangkhuls are also known as 'Wung' before its term is coins. In most of their writings, the term 'Wung' is used as a prefix before the word Tangkhul. The term 'Wung' is also known by other terms like hong, hung, and hwung which means people or folk belonging to a regal family.[20]

---

[20] Mawon Somingam, Understanding the Origin of the terms 'WUNG', 'HAO' and 'TANGKHUL', Vol. 3(5), 36-40, May (2014), International Research Journal of Social Sciences, ISSN 2319–3565.

The Tangkhul community celebrates several festivals, including Luira Phanit (Seed Sowing Festival), Yarra (Youth Festival), Mangkhap Phanit (Completion of Rice Transplantation Festival), Chumpha Phanit (Festival of Thanksgiving for the New Harvest) and Thisam Phanit (Farewell Festival to the Spirit of the Dead). In the Northern Zone (Raphei) of the Ukhrul District, Shinat Phanit is celebrated, particularly in Lunghar village and its neighboring villages, during March and April. In the olden days, during Shinat, animal blood was used to rinse agricultural tools to cleanse them and prevent injury, as well as to encourage more of a harvest. Locals also bake traditional bread during this festival. In Lunghar village, it is also synonymously called 'Bread Festival' due to the abundance of bread. While non-traditional festivals like Shirui Lily Festival (State flower festival) celebrated in May and Kachai Lemon Festival celebrated in January have taken center stage due to their significance and value to the Tangkhul community, other well-known festivals are Sirarakhong Hathei Phanit (Chilli Festival) celebrated in August and Shuri Kaso Phanat (Garlic festival) at Talui village celebrated in April. In Marem village, Machee Ru (Indigenous Salt Spring) festival has recently started among many other festivals.

Tangkhul community is one of the most distinct tribes in Manipur; they follow the strict law and order given by the village elders. They belong to the head-hunting group and are very brave in warfare. Until the arrival of an American Baptist Missionary William Pettigrew to Ukhrul in 1896, they remained aggressive toward the other groups of the community. They are the first ever tribe to convert to Christianity in Manipur. Since then the Tangkhul villages began embracing Christianity and were growing exponentially, eventually leading to the conversion of the entire Tangkhul community into Christianity. Therefore, Christian ethics and moral values have a very strong influence on the life of Tangkhul in the present.

William Pettigrew brought Western education to the area of Ukhrul district, inhabited Tangkhul tribe. This brought drastic changes in the culture, religion, politics, occupation, dress, and way of living of the Tangkhul tribe. The contemporary Tangkhul community has undergone significant changes, adopting Western culture and education in various social aspects. Western culture has influenced every facet of life, resulting in shifts in language and beliefs. Unlike the Tangkhuls of the past, today's generation has embraced these changes, yet the core Tangkhul identity remains steadfast from generation to generation.

Ukhrul District

Ukhrul District (currently including Kamjong District) was officially declared on 15th July 1983, after Chandel District was carved out from Manipur East District and the title of the district was changed to Ukhrul District. The Tangkhul forms the majority ethnic group in this district. The area of the Ukhrul district is 4,544 Sq. Km. Ukhrul district lies in the north-eastern corner of Manipur and it extends between a Latitude of 24^0 N-25.41^0 N and a Longitude of 94^0 E-94.47^0 E. The climatic condition of Ukhrul is Maximum: 33^0 C and Minimum: 3^0 C. The Average Annual rainfall is 1763.7 mm. Ukhrul is linked with Imphal, the state capital by NH 150 about 84 Km.

As per the 2011 census, the total population of Ukhrul District is 1,83,998, of which the male population is 94718 and the female population is 89280, with a Sex Ratio of 948 females for every 1000 males. The total Literacy rate is 81.35%; the Male Literacy Rate is 85.25% and Female Literacy Rate is 76.95%. The total no. of Households is 35,694 and the total no. of inhabited Villages is 213. The Ukhrul District (including Kamjong District) has 7 (Seven) Sub-Divisions which are co-terminus with the 8(Eight) Development Blocks. Jessami was a part of the Chingai block and Sahamphung was a part of Kamjong block. There are three Assembly Constituencies in Ukhrul(i) 43- Phungyar (ST) AC, (ii) 44- Ukhrul (ST) AC, and (iii) 45 - Chingai (ST) AC.

11

METHODOLOGY

Universe of the Study

The finding is exclusive of the Tangkhul communities residing in Ukhrul and Kamjong districts of Manipur. Kamjong District was carved out from Ukhrul District on 8th December 2016, which has not been recognized by the United Naga Council (UNC), and the matter is still in court.

The study of the population is confined to Ukhrul district, including Kamjong, in Manipur state. The area of the districts is 4,544 sq. km, with a household population of 35,614 (2011 Census).

Methods of Sample Selection

Morgan and Krejcie methods of population study were used for sample selection. The total households of the seven selected villages from four blocks are counted to be 7827. Considering a large number of families, the researcher adopted Morgan and Krejcie method and selected 391 families.

Steps 1. The researcher selected four blocks where the highest human rights violation was recorded so far by purposive sampling methods.

Step 2. The researcher also considered the villages of the selected blocks where the highest human rights violation was recorded so far by using simple random sampling methods and selected 5% of families from each village.

Table no. A

No. of Blocks, Villages, Household and Sample size of 5% (According to Morgan and Krejcie formula.)

Sl. No.	Blocks	Total no. of villages	No. of household	Selected villages		Sample size of 5%
				Village	No of Household	
1	Ukhrul	41	13668	Ukhrul (Urban)	5226	261
				Huining	688	34
2	Chingai	27	6102	Jessami	558	28
				2. Huishu	201	10
3	Lungchong Meiphei	28	7073	Talui	820	41
				Ngainga	267	13
4	Phungyar	37	3323	Kumrum	67	4
Total	4 Blocks			7 villages	7827	391

Sample Size

There are 391 samples from the seven most violated villages which were selected from four different blocks of Ukhrul district (NPMHR court referred data and News Papers Archive).

Table no. B

No. of Villages and Respondents

Name of Village	No. of Respondents	Percent
Huining	34	8.7
Huishu	10	2.6
Hunphun	261	66.8
Jessami	28	7.2
Kumram	4	1.0
Ngainga	13	3.3
Talui	41	10.5
Total	391	100.0

Data Analysis

Analysis of the data is conducted concerning the data collected from various constituencies and has been subjected to verification, quantification, and coding by referring to a coding key. The coded data is entered into the computer for data processing and analysis. Statistical Package for Social Sciences (SPSS) is used to calculate percentile, frequency distribution table, cross-tabulation, and chi-square test to draw inferences and justify the findings.

12

HUMAN RIGHTS VIOLATION IN THE SELECTED VILLAGES

Ukhrul district is well-known for its gross violations of the law, and many of the worst incidents of human rights violations have occurred in Ukhrul town, Huining village, Talui village, Ngainga village, Kumrum village, Jessami village, and Huishu village. These villages have unjustly suffered various gross human rights violations for no reason, and their cries for justice have still not been addressed by the State Government. To date, the government has provided little to no assistance for the violations committed by the Indian Armed Forces, despite the need for rehabilitation for these villages for the losses caused by the Armed Forces. These villages have been struggling for years, bearing the scars of violence and waiting for justice, yet they still seem to be a distant dream.

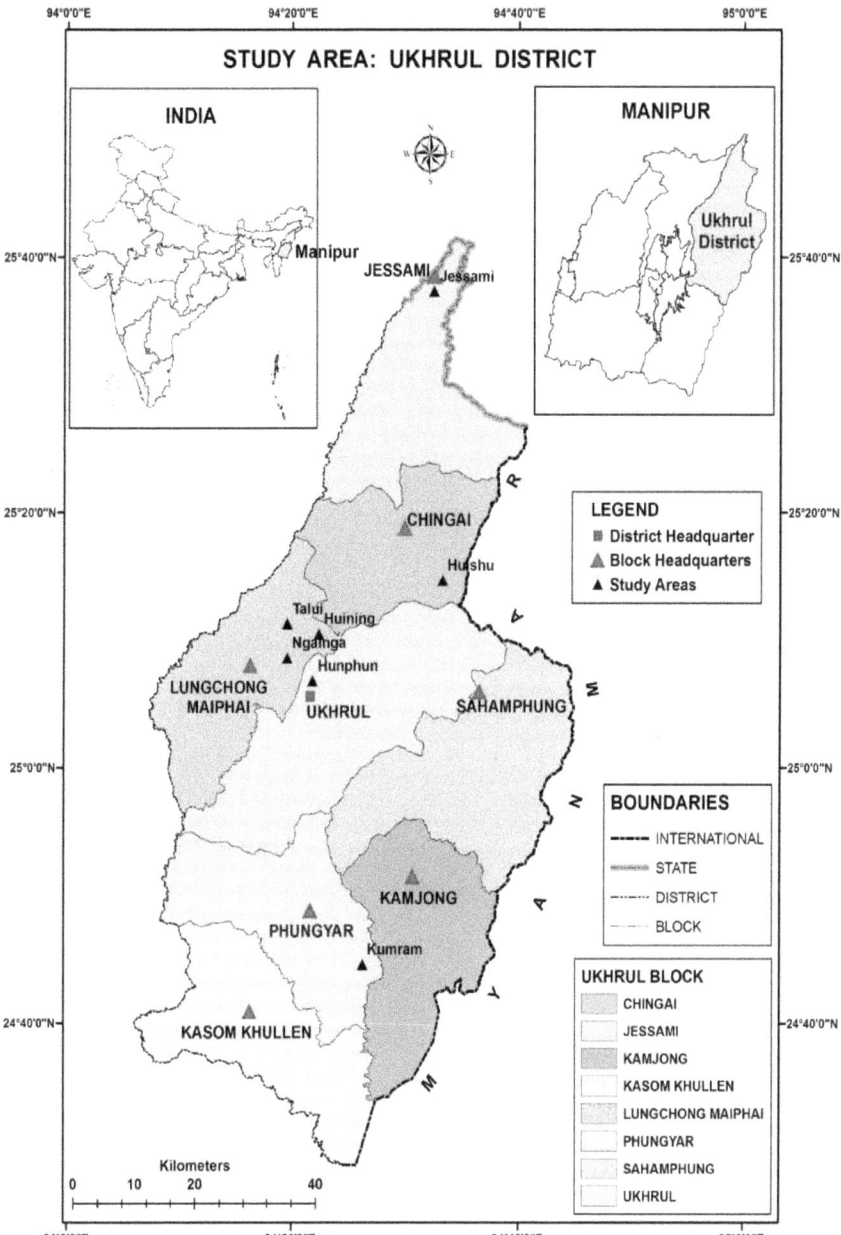

Map Showing Indian state and selected villages of the study[21]

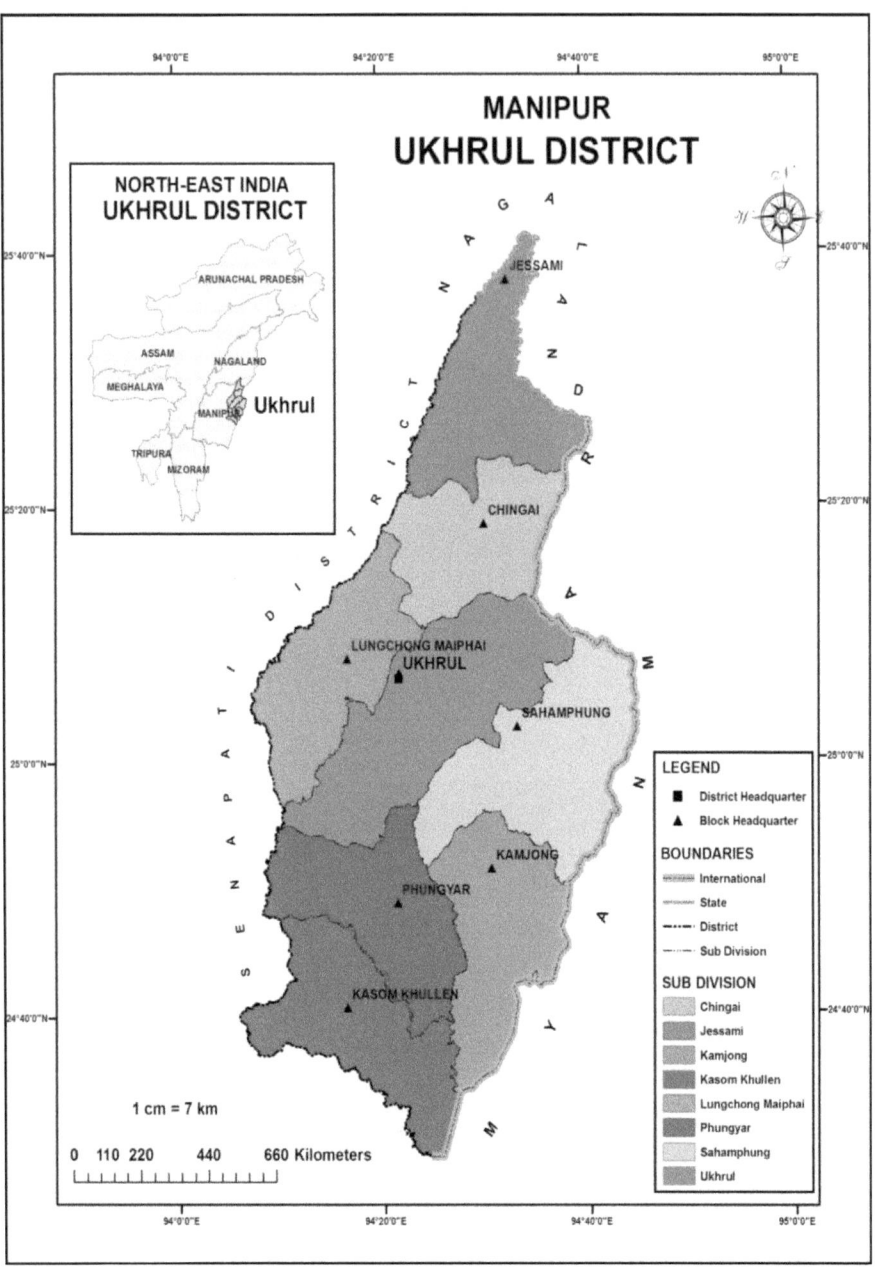

---

[21] Jashua Kazingmei M.A in GIS and M.A in Geography

Map showing the Northeastern States and selected areas of the study.[22]

While attempting to demolish and capture Paosaitarung post, one of the well-established NSCN (IM) camps located between Ngainga village and Talui village, in 1966, the Indian army lost several soldiers. In their aggravated anger, with wild intentions, the Indian Army planned to demolish Talui village on 24th February 1968. The Indian Army had taken permission and an order was given by the centre to destroy Talui village. The Talui village youth happened to perform a traditional dance at Somdal village Golden Jubilee that year. Lt. Col. Rantawala, present at the occasion, was impressed by the beautiful traditional dance performed by the Talui youths. On humanity grounds, Lt. Col. Rantawala revealed the attack planned on Talui village by the Indian Army. Instantly, on hearing the news of the imminent planned attack, the village elders and the responsible leaders went and discussed with the NSCN (IM) cadres to evacuate Talui Torei Kachiw camp and Prao camp with due concern for the villagers. The NSCN (IM) evacuated Talui village for the goodwill of the villagers. After finding out that the NSCN (IM) had evacuated people from Talui village, the Indian Army stopped the terror attack planned on Talui village.[23]

On 27th February 1966, along with the Home Guard, the Indian Army fiercely attacked Paosaitarung post and banished the NSCN (IM) from the camp. After dispersing all the NSCN (IM), the Indian Army dismantled and burned down Paosaitarung post. The Indian Army burst out their anger at the Ngainga villagers and blazed 70 houses in Ngainga. They even set the granaries on fire where the villagers stored their food grains. Dresses, ornaments, and other precious goods were taken away by the Home Guard. In another incident in the same year on 23rd December 1966, the brutal Indian Army (CRPF) came to the village again and burned down the village for the second time, including Ngainga M.E School. Only teachers' quarters and 10 houses were held back to set up their posts and live among the villagers, treating them inhumanely, resulting in the fleeing of many villagers. That year, the villagers celebrated Christmas Eve in the forest led by Pastor K. Rasheng, the villagers still cannot forget the cruel tragic experience. In another inhuman incident, Ngainga Post Commander Luit.

---

[22] Jashua Kazingmei M.A in GIS and M.A in Geography (JNU)
[23] Indo-Naga Rairei Wung Regionna ngarara kahai Thotchan. Published by Talui Ex-NNC/FGN Workers' Long 2012

Dubey, Mahar Regt. and Phungyar Post Commander Capt. Mandhir Singh, Madras Regt. attempted to rape Ms. Luingamla Muinao, an eighth-standard student. But on failing to rape her, the two Indian Army officers shot her to death with a pistol on 24th January 1986.[24]

On March 4, 1974, Ms. Rose Ningshen, a student of Phungyar High School, was raped by BSF (Border Security Force) officials; Major Bundhir, Dharma Prakash, and Captain Negy, who were posted in her village Kumrum. The BSF officers singled out only the females in the village to help them arrange their accommodation, fetch water, and prepare groceries for them. After two days after the rape incident, Rose Ningshen committed suicide due to shameful and disgraceful humiliation. Till today, Rose Ningshen has been denied justice. It has now been more than 40 years of fighting for her rights but justice is still awaited. A series of protests and appeals have been made but all have gone in vain, so Rose remains helpless and silent in her grave, longing for justice. [25] Other rape incidents also happened in Grihang village near Rose Ningshen's village and they were committed by the same BSF officers.

Huining, which is 20 km away from Ukhrul headquarter, was raided by Sikh Battalion at 8 p.m. on 5th March 1982 in search of NSCN suspects. The womenfolk were forcibly taken into the village church and were not allowed to leave until the next day. K. Rashing, a tall man of age 30, was taken away to the Army post to be interrogated. He was taken to the central camp at Leimakhong near Imphal for questioning. It lasted 41 days, and he was given the worst kind of treatment, including electric shocks all over his body, even in the private parts. Most of the time, he was hung upside down, thrashed on his soles with lathis, and chili powder was pushed into his rectum. But even after several painful torments, he was found to be innocent. However, four days after Rashing was arrested, the Indian Army came back to Huining village and forcefully blindfolded and took C. Paul, asst. Pastor of Halang Baptist church, and C. Daniel, headmaster of the Government High School. They were beaten harshly and were forced to sign on a blank paper and then they were forcibly attested by C. Shangnam

---

[24] Ngainga Shanao Long Silver Jubilee 2012, THOTCHAN, published by History committee Ngainga Shanao Long.
[25] Revisiting Rape Victim Rose Ningshen 43 Years Later, The Sangai Express, 12 May 2017

and H.L. Machihan, two village leaders. After their forced disappearance on 10th March 1982, C. Paul and C. Daniel did not return home but the army informed their wives that they had released them the very next day. To date, nobody knows their whereabouts.[26]

On 11th March 1996, following the attack, the Assam Rifles personnel set on fire the entire village (Huishu village) of 153 houses after looting and raiding all the precious things in the sack. After that, the Assam Rifles brutally tortured the villagers and fired bullets blindly, which resulted in the killing of three villagers on the spot due to bullet wounds. Moreover, the womenfolk were used as a shield by the Assam Rifles personnel. The helpless Huishu villagers went and hid in the nearby villages for their safety but many landed in the jungle as the roadway was blocked by the Assam Rifles personnel.

On 2nd October 1996, The 5th Sikh Light Infantry rushed to Jessami village, situated in the north of Manipur, bordering Nagaland. They assembled all the villagers and forcefully detained them for two continuous days. Most of the villagers were viciously beaten up and a pregnant woman and three others were molested in front of all the villagers. A few villagers were inside the church for the worship service but Captain Ashwin furiously entered the church and went directly to the pulpit with his pistol pointing to the worshippers and shouted, "Stop praying and chanting, or else I will shoot you!" Inside the church, men and women were forcefully separated. After some time, a Nepali was brought to the church and everybody was checked one by one by the Armed forces. Unfortunately, one person happened to be from another village (Talloi), and out of suspicion, he was beaten up brutally in front of all the worshippers inside the church. Another two visitors hailing from Kachai village were forcefully taken back to the Army camp and were tortured brutally. They were handed back to Jessami village authority, but one of them could not even walk because of the brutal torture.

7th July 1997 incident; when some suspected NSCN members fired at Assam Rifle vehicles at a place popularly known as Ukhrul viewpoint Awungtang, a heavy reinforcement swooped upon the civil population. The spot and nearby houses bore a good number of bullet marks, which only

---

[26] India Today,Inputs & source: http://indiatoday.intoday.in/.../war-rages-inte.../1/392479.html

testify to the number of rounds fired indiscriminately by Assam Rifles, the so-called Friends of the Hill People. The Assam Rifles personnel started beating and dragging off any civilian they found on the road, lanes, by-lanes, and even in their own houses. Some teachers and students of Savio School were beaten black and blue and many victims had to be hospitalized. About 95 civilians had lodged FIRs with the Ukhrul Police Station. Mr. Rammaso Shingnaisui was tortured to death in the 20 Assam Rifles custody. Later, it was handed into the Ukhrul Police Station after much pressure from the public and civil administration. The Govt. of Manipur declared in the Assembly to commission a judicial inquiry on the incident but has not initiated it so far. Sporadic house raids were conducted by the AR personnel at night and during daytime as well in Wino bazaar, Viewland, Phungreitang, and the 7th Finance Quarters, in which no arrest could be made but fear was generated and inconveniences were caused to the inmates of those houses.

Non-disbursement of employees' pay at Ukhrul headquarters; all of a sudden, Armed AR personnel entered the police station where salaries for Govt. employees were disbursed during the first week of June for the month of May 2000. The cashiers of all the department offices were made to recount the currencies in different denominations, to show exact numbers and the actual amount of each employee. The cashiers of offices reported the matter to the Deputy Commissioner (District Magistrate). It was learned that D.C. had issued an order to the Assam Rifles to stop it. But, instead of complying with the order of the District Magistrate, the Assam Rifles Personnel forced each Govt. employee to collect their salary by themselves. So every month, employees from all parts of the district had to come to Ukhrul headquarter, wasting five working days. Doctors, medical personnel, and teachers had to leave their wards unattended for two to five days each month.

Section 144 of the Criminal Procedure Code (S.144 CrPC) was enforced in Ukhrul on the 13th of July 2014 after the killing of Mr. Ngalangzar Malue (aged 60), one of the members of the Autonomous District Council (ADC) near Finch Corner by unidentified gunmen. After the incident, Ukhrul District and the entire adjoining areas were heavily militarized by deploying hundreds of State Armed Forces; Police Commando, and Indian Reserve Batallion (IRB). In protest of the enforcement of (S.144 CrPC) the

Tangkhul community organized a Peace Rally against the imposition of Section 144 CrPC in Ukhrul district headquarters on 30th August 2014. Manipur police commandos opened fire on the unarmed peaceful protesters, killing two innocent civilians, Ramkashing Vashi (aged 26), and Mayopam Ramror (aged 31) on the spot and several people were wounded, including women.

The police rained tear gas, smoke bombs, and bullets on the crowd, resulting in loss of life and plunging the entire town into chaos. The entire town was taken hostage and the State government blamed the citizens, due to which normal life and public tranquility were shaken. People became panicked and insecure for fear of what might happen in the future in the long run. Through democratic and peaceful means, people have been protesting and appealing to the authorities since July 13, 2014, yet there has been no response. The public and civil organizations in the district have been telling the Government that there is no law and regulation in Ukhrul town. The State Government refused to listen and insisted on prolonging the siege instead. Tangkhul community has suffered enough and shed enough blood as the Police Commandos and State government have committed enough gross violations of the law.[27]

---

[27] Change.org, Themmarak kapai; "Petitioning Narendra Modi, Hon'ble Prime Minister of India"

13

HUMAN RIGHTS VIOLATION INCIDENTS IN UKHRUL DISTRICT[28]

Ukhrul district is entirely a rural area inhabited by the Tangkhul community since time immemorial. It is one of the hill districts of Manipur state. Tangkhul community is a cultural tribe known for its beautiful and unique culture. They follow Christianity and speak Tangkhul language, which is originally a Hunphun dialect. Agriculture is the main occupation and source of livelihood for the Tangkhul community. The district is rich with a variety of flora and fauna. The beautiful Shirui lily, which only grows in the hill range of Shirui Kashong is the state flower of Manipur. The Tangkhul community is simple and kind-hearted in nature; they have their own unique customary laws that safeguard their identity and goodwill.

Whereas, the imposition of AFSPA 1958 and Section 144 of the Criminal Procedure Code has provoked violence and social tension throughout the Ukhrul district. Once a peaceful area, Ukhrul has now become a land of bloodshed and human rights violations. The first incident of mass punishment was recorded in 1963; four villages of Tangkhul community, namely Talui village, Tusom village, Sirarakhong village, and Sinakeithei village were collectively fined under sub-section (1) of section 2 of the West Bengal Collective Fine Act, 1950 (West Bengal Act XXXIX of 1950) on the pretext Harboring Naga Goondas, supplying food and money to them, allowing free movement in their village areas, failing to give information about their movement, and rendering assistance to the "Naga Goondas." Talui village was collectively fined Rs. 25000 whereas Tusom village, Sirarakhong village, and Sinakeithei village were collectively fined Rs. 20000 each as punishment for giving alms to the so-called "Naga Goondas" by the Armed Forces. The villagers had to sell their domestic

---

[28] Pending cases of Naga People Movement for Human Rights

animals, ancestral plots, cultivated land, and privately owned forested plots. The Indian Armed Forces even threatened to set their villages on fire. All the villagers, young and old, were pulled down to the village playground and tortured mercilessly without any reason.[29] Nobody came to rescue the villagers and despite false accusations by the Indian Armed Forces, the four villages were not given any assistance from the State government to rehabilitate them.

The United Nations (UN) had a written prohibition on human rights violations in Naga Hills from 23rd December 1957. A fact-finding team of civil rights leaders came to Delhi from Nagalim. They included Ms. Nanditat Haksar and Ms. Urmila Phadvisa of the People's Union for Democratic Rights (PUDR), Ms. Premila Dandavate from Mahila Makshita Samiti (MMS) and Kirti Singh of Janwadi Mahila Samite (JMS). They composed the civil rights team that visited Nagalim and reported the truth they found. Unfortunately, the Government remained silent on all the points of torture of men and women, rape of women, harassment of school children, teachers, government servants, church leaders, businessmen, and misappropriation of civilian savings, crops, and personal properties.

February 1966: Under the command of Chaudhoury, Indian troops arrested Mr. Mw. Tuimayang (aged 40) (Runa Poeyu 1965-66) a village authority (VA), s/o Mw. Ngakapthi and Ms. Zangaila of Tushen Chanhong Village, Ukhrul. He was being dragged from one army post to another crossing Lamlang Gate, Pharung, Seikhor, Teinem, Champhung, Tora, Maichon, Kachai, and lastly Talui Army Headquarters. He was beaten black and blue for a week and jailed for months.

Later, on one of the prison days, Army commander Chaudhoury said, "I have received many reports against you from your villagers, but I found no evidence against you. You are innocent. Will you file a complaint to any court against me for the torture you went through?" At this, Mr. Tuimayang said, "Saab! I will not file any case against you, but let God judge those who tried to violate my innocence". Tuimayang was released from custody that evening. He reached his village around midnight. Though he was tortured for weeks, he felt no pain or sickness in his body. He praised God

---

[29] Naga Army Paosaitarung, 1966. Published by Wung Naga Army, Federal Government of Nagaland (FGN)

for the miracle that happened to him. Thus, he expressed the greatness and love of God.

1960-68: Indian troops, including the Assam Rifles, Manipur Rifles, and Manipur Home Guard, completely incinerated several villages. Among them were Khangkhui, Ngainga, Lungshang, Nambashi, Khonglo, Huishu, and numerous other villages, the details of which remain undocumented.

1963-67: In Lunghar village, instead of searching for the Naga Army in the jungle, there were reports of the Indian Army, Assam Rifles, Manipur Rifles, and Manipur Home Guard subjecting villagers to dreadful torture, which tragically led to fatalities. In 1965, the entire village was reportedly set ablaze, and domestic animals were also reported to have been killed.

Some of the victims were:

1. Hs. Mishivam	2. Hs. Mikzo	3. Hs. Reoza
4. Hs. Areithei	5. Hs. Kahaosan	6. Hs. Thuingaleng
7. Hs. Ruichumhao	8. Hs. Luishom	9. Hs. Maiming
10. Gh. Maya	11. Gh. Sharei	12. Gh. Luitong
13. Gh. Malungring	14. Gh. Theikhaning	15. Lw. Pilei
16. Lw. Wungkhaleng	17. Lw. Sãra	18. Th. Shukemla
19. Th. Mingthing	20. K. Yangshi	21. K. Ronhung
22. M. Saitui	23. As. Reoza	

Khanang A. Shishak s/o Ralo A. Shishak and Kareila A. Shishak of Shangshak, were arrested from their village by Igarh Regiment 25 personnel under the command of Captain Sharma (1967). Along with them, As. Kashikui, M. Ramlung, Ramso Ragui and As. Kashikui were arrested but later As. Kashikui was released and within no time they were taken to the army post of Lungshang and then Tashar. They endured three days of brutal torture, harassment, and electric shocks, leaving them half-dead. Later, they were brought to Shangshak.

Rape cases and abuse:

Ms. Rose Ningshen D/O Honaprang of Ngaprum (Kumram) village a student of Phungyar High School committed suicide after she was repeatedly raped by (BSF) Border Security Force officials namely: 1. Major Bundhir, 2. Dharma Prakash, 3. Captain Negy in March 1974. An FIR of the case bearing No. 4(3)74 U/S 376/201 IPC was registered.

The 9th Battalion BSF officers raped Ms. Rose Ningshen on 4th March 1974. The incident happened when Kumram youths were practicing songs for the special festival of their village. Suddenly, more than 500 BSF personnel came to Kumram village searching for the Naga Insurgents. The BSF officers chose four girls from the group, including Ms. Rose Ningshen, to help the BSF officers in arranging accommodation. The BSF officers asked the three other girls to get other bedding materials but Ms. Rose Ningshen was made to do the household tasks. Knowing that the three females had gone, the three officers took advantage of her being alone and raped her. Due to the humiliation of the rape incident, she committed suicide after two days by hanging herself in the kitchen with the suicide note written in Tangkhul dialect.

Between the 3rd to 6th of March, other incidents took place in another village. Officials of the same 9th Battalion (BSF) Border Security Force namely:

1. Major Bundhir, 2. Captain Negy, 3. Major Dharam Prakash, 4. Sub-Major Bhagwan Singh, 5. Inspector Jet Singh, 6. Havaldar Chandra Singh, 7. L/NK. Men Bahadur, and their Sepoys resorted to mass rape at Grihang village. The victims are 1. Ms. Ngaishengla aged 23, 2. Ms. Shiningla, and 3. Ms. Paothingla. The incident was registered under FIR. No.3 (3) 74. Naga People's Movement of Human Rights and other civil organizations have appealed to the state government and central government but got no positive result or response.

Record of 1980-1982 incidents:

In 1980: Captain NL Sharma, the post commander of 20 Assam Rifles in Kuingai village, Ukhrul District, allegedly molested village girls in the military doctor's room. The girls had reportedly gone there upon the invitation of the wife of the said doctor. When the girls ran home, Captain NL Sharma followed them with several security personnel. Upon reaching the village, the Captain reportedly broke into houses in search of one of the girls. Eventually, he found the girl and ordered everyone to leave while pulling her inside an empty room in a house. The owner of the house, who had been pushed out, held on to the girl and tried to free her at the risk of his own life. Several elders of the village were beaten up while attempting to free the girl during the night. Later, Kongsui Luithui, the Chairman of the Autonomous District Council, took up the matter with higher authorities.

19th April 1981: On the night of April 19, 1981, around 8:10 pm, Captain NL Sharma, fully armed but dressed in civilian attire, entered the residence of Kongsui Luithui accompanied by two armed jawans. They forcibly dragged him and his wife out of their home blindfolded Kongsui Luithui, and threatened to kill him. They intimidated both him and his family members. He recalled the incidents in which he was involved, specifically, Mr. Luithui taking a public stand against the molestation and attempted rape of two women by Capt. Sharma in 1979 at Kuingai village. Additionally, Mr. Luithui opposed the firing at point-blank range at Mr. Moon K. Shimray, a Town Committee Member, carried out by Major Sharawat, 2nd in Command of 20 AR. Capt. Sharma cited these cases as defamation against him, asserting that he was an all-powerful first-class gazetted officer who could only be dismissed by the President of India.

He also misrepresented the ruling party; claiming that he was following the wishes of Congress and that since Mr. Luithui was in the opposition, Sharma could do anything to him, even kill him with impunity. Despite appeals from family members, he carried Mr. Luithui in a Jeep to an isolated place about 7 km away from his home. He was brutally assaulted and tortured for nearly two hours. Several times, Sharma attempted to shoot him and make it appear as though he was killed in self-defense by placing a country-made pistol beside Mr. Luithui, but the jawans did not cooperate. It was only when Mr. Luithui's family members could inform the Commanding Officer of 20 AR through the Police that he was released the next morning at 2:30 am in a semi-conscious state by the C.O. 20 AR, who stated that he had Capt. Sharma under house arrest.

20th February 1982: After horrible harassment at Paorei Village by 21st Sikh Regiment, some 11 young and beautiful maidens were picked up by the army and were taken away to the jungle to satisfy their nasty and beastly lust. **20th February 1982:** In the village of Kalhang, the residents endured severe harassment, with six young girls publicly molested and forcibly taken to the Awang Kasom Army post. After approximately two weeks of detention, during which they suffered further abuse at the hands of the Regiment members, the girls were eventually sent back home, grappling with psychosis and burdened by profound mental traumas. Their lives thereafter were marked by disgrace and enduring societal stigma.

21st February 1982: This kind of torture emphasized the plight of individuals caught between the Naga Army and the Indian Army. The case of Mr. Sãra from Lunghar serves as a poignant illustration of this harrowing predicament. Mr. Sãra's brother, Mr. Shatnam, joined the NSCN, leading to the apprehension of Mr. Sãra, his son, Mr. Ngachonmi, and his elder brother, Wungkhaleng, along with Wungkhaleng's son, Ningreion, all taken from Lunghar. They were arbitrarily taken to Longpi Post for interrogation.

During the interrogation, they endured kicks from several jawans and merciless flogging, followed by electric shocks to their private parts. Sadly, none were spared except for Mr. Wungkhaleng. This incident marked the second instance of Mr. Sãra enduring brutal torture, the first occurring in the incident of 1965. The repeated torture significantly deteriorated his health, leading to his admission to Imphal Hospital, where he underwent treatment for over a month. Ultimately, they were released after interrogation, as no evidence was found regarding Mr. Shatnam's whereabouts. Regrettably, due to the lasting impact on their health, all three individuals who were subjected to brutal beatings were unable to perform strenuous jobs.

26th February 1982: Just a month after Mrs. K. Levis married Mr. T. Vareichung on January 24, 1982, the 21st Sikh Regiment descended upon Nungbi village. They forcibly entered the house of T. Ronhung, where T. Vareichung was having dinner with three friends. All four were taken at gunpoint and compelled to lie down. Subsequently, 20 jawans beat them with rifle butts, firewood, and a dao. No reasons were given for this brutal treatment, and the victims were left lying there. Mrs. K. Levis nursed her husband for 20 days, but unfortunately, he did not recover. The family then decided to take him to Ukhrul District Hospital, which, regrettably, lacked the necessary equipment to handle such a severe case, prompting a transfer to Imphal. There, an X-ray revealed damage beyond healing to his liver, lungs, heart, and stomach. He was brought home on July 17, 1982.

26th February 1982: Mrs. Hormila recounted the tragic story of her husband, Mr. Yarphui, a resident of Marangphung Village in Ukhrul. On

February 26, 1982, while traveling from his village to Ukhrul in a truck with fellow villagers, their journey was abruptly halted by the military. The men were subjected to severe beatings, and as a result, Mr. Yarphui had to be hospitalized in Imphal. Suffering from extensive swelling throughout his body, he ultimately succumbed to a serious injury on July 1, 1982. According to Mrs. Hormila, her husband's untimely demise was a result of what she perceived as an act of vengeance for the death of soldiers. Left alone with her four children, Mrs. Hormila found herself in a precarious situation, without any means to support her grieving family.

5th March 1982: Ms. Thanmila, 26 years old, from Paorei Village in Ukhrul District, recounted a harrowing experience where the army compelled villagers to provide thatch for their camp without any compensation for the thatch or the labor. On the day of the military operation, she was weeding the garden when a jawan appeared. Since her house was far away, she did not hear the army coming. The jawan pinned her down to the ground and pulled at her lungi, he tried to tuck between her legs and tried to rape her. In distress, she screamed for her husband, whom she believed to be inside their home. He emerged but stood shocked and helpless. At that moment, another jawan appeared and signaled to the first to hurry and collect the people at the playground.

6th March 1982: At Phungcham village, PR. Machihan said that 2 jawans burst into his bedroom and pulled his wife out of the bed by her hair. He flashed a torch on their faces and they were told to go to the playground. He also heard the cry of his neighbor Ms. L. Langaila, a widow. He rushed to her house and found a jawan who had his arms around her waist and was pulling her by the hair as she cried out in pain. He told the jawan in Manipuri that he would inform the higher authorities. They left her and went into P. Hangmila's house and tried the same thing with her friend Ms. Alice. The next day, PR. Machihan was severely beaten up by the jawans for trying to help these women.

25th February 1982: Three women from Nungbi village Ukhrul District, namely Ruth, Chanreiphy, and Zingnimla told that they were forced by the 21st Sikh Regiment personnel to lift their lungis to expose their private parts. They expressed how frightened they were to discuss the incident.

6th March 1982: The Headman of Phungcham Village said that he had been picked up by the 21st Sikh Regiment on 6th March 1982 and brought to the 20 AR camp, Ukhrul. He was blindfolded and ordered to strip his clothes.

He was severely beaten, kicked brutally, and told to confess that he knew the whereabouts of the Naga Army. When he said that he knew nothing he was given electric shock on his thumb five or six times. He was later handed over to the Police at Ukhrul.

March 1982: At Lunghar Village, Mr. Sirapui and Mr. Sharei, teachers of Lunghar Junior Primary School narrated that they were tortured. Mr. Siraphui related the story that he was picked up and severely beaten. Mr. Sharei also shared that he was taken from his village in the third week of May by 20 AR personnel without any reason. He was kept in a trench at Longpi post without any clothes. The next day, he was taken to Somsai 20 AR camp Ukhrul and put into a trench for another two days and two nights.

4th March 1982: Mr. S.A. Peter, a contractor from Huishu village, was arrested along with eight others while en route to Ukhrul. Among them were a jawan of Assam Rifles on leave and some school children. The perpetrators tied him up and subjected him to brutal beatings on the soles of his feet. The assault was so severe that he could no longer walk. The medical treatment expenses amounted to about Rs. 6,000. To cover these costs, his wife had to borrow money from various people. Mr. Peter was one of the eight individuals who suffered a similar type of torture. Additionally, Mr. Wungazai was given an electric shock in his private area, and hot water was forcefully poured into his nose.

3rd March 1982: Pastor Athei Mashangva of Huishu Baptist Church Ukhrul District reported that he was arrested on 3rd March by 20 Assam Rifles and taken to Poi village and then to Chingai village Army Post, where the 21st Sikh Regiment personnel took him to their camp the next morning. He was severely beaten and pushed into a bunker. In his statement, he said, "The bunker was so small that I couldn't bend but then two personnel jumped over my back and started shoving me inside, stamping all the way. I was then hung upside down and they started beating the soles of my feet mercilessly. My hands were tied, and my mouth gagged while they applied electric current over the ears and mouth."

22nd February to March 1982: Mr. S. Mahuiri, an ex-pastor of Kalhang village in Ukhrul District, was taken into custody on 22nd February by the 21st Sikh Regiment at Awang Kasom Post. Subsequently, he endured severe beatings at the post and was instructed to undress and raise his arms. However, due to the severity of the beating, he was unable to comply. The jawan demanded that he reveal his worst injury, and when Mr. Mahuiri showed it, the jawan poked him with his fist at that spot, causing him to lose consciousness. The torture persisted until 3rd March. Later, he was handed over to the Ukhrul police, and the Magistrate directed his transfer to a hospital for medical attention.

Reverend Makanmi Rimai, the ex-secretary of Tangkhul Naga Baptist Convention (TNBC), also suffered severe beatings. He recounted that on 13th August 1982, the army compelled the pastor of Tora village to open the church for their use as a camp. Reverend Rimai was outraged by the army's disregard for the sanctity of the church, treating it as a public hall rather than a holy place, a situation he found intolerable.

Enforced disappearance of Assistant Pastor and High School Headmaster:

C. Paul Assistant pastor of Huining village and Mr. C. Daniel, Headmaster of Junior High School Huining village were kidnapped on 10th March 1982 by the 21st Sikh Regiment and went missing. Writ Petition (Cr) NO. 148 of 1983 Supreme Court of India directed the S.P of Police Ukhrul to commence the investigation. Mr. C. Paul and Mr. C. Daniel were forcefully taken to Phungrei Camp from Huining village by the 21st Sikh Regiment Officer-in-charge. They were not allowed to communicate with anyone, and thereafter their whereabouts were not made known.

On 5th March 1982, the 21st Sikh Regiment raided Huining village, surrounding the villagers. Later, on 6th March 1982, the villagers were released after enduring harsh detention for a whole day. Some of the jawans forcefully obtained signatures from the village headman, Mr. Machihan, and Mr. Shangam (Village Authority Members). The next day, Mr. Machihan reported this inhuman act to the Deputy Commissioner. However, Mr. C. Daniel and Mr. C. Paul did not return. Consequently, their wives went to inquire about their husbands' whereabouts at Phungrei Army camp. While waiting, they witnessed their husbands being taken away by the Armed forces in the west direction. The villagers and the village headman filed a written complaint against the 21st Sikh Regiment with the Deputy Commissioner for the incident that occurred in the village. Additionally, the villagers filed a complaint about the issuance of the certificate by the Armed forces, claiming the release of Mr. C. Daniel and Mr. C. Paul in the presence of all the villagers on 11th March 1982.

With the order of the Deputy Commissioner, the Superintendent of Police conducted an inquiry into the complaint by the villagers. The report was then sent to the Chief Secretary of the State, stating that the information in the report about the release of Mr. C. Daniel and Mr. C. Paul was incorrect, as the two had not yet returned to their village. In response to the complainant's notice, the Armed forces asserted that the two missing individuals were taken to Phungrei camp on 10th March 1982 to identify some suspects. Both of them were held at Phungrei camp that night and were released the next day in the presence of the village headman and Mr. Shangam, who were friends of the missing individuals. The Armed forces claimed no knowledge of the whereabouts of the two missing people after that. The Armed Forces denied that the wives of the missing individuals visited the Army camp on 11th March 1982. Additionally, the Armed Forces rejected the assertion that they obtained forced signatures on a blank piece of paper from the village headman and other villagers.

The Armed Forces asserted that Mr. C. Daniel and Mr. C. Paul, the two missing individuals, came to the Army camp at the request of the Armed Forces authority. However, both were released at the request of the villagers. The Armed Forces claimed that both of them departed from the Army camp accompanied by some of the villagers.

Killed after rape attempt on Ms. Luingamla Muinao:

Among the many stories is the story of Ms. Luingamla Muinao, a fifteen-year-old girl from Ngainga village, whom an Indian soldier Capt. Mandhir Singh and Lt. Sanjeev Dubey shot dead on 24th Jan 1986 because she resisted their attempt to rape her. As she resisted with all her might and valor, Capt. Mandhir Singh pulled out his pistol and shot her dead in cold blood. She was alone at her home, weaving a shawl in the afternoon when these two Army officers barged in and assaulted her. Zamthingla Ruivah, a teenage neighbor, was apparently close by when the incident happened, but she was terrified and helpless.

In fact, the two officers visited Ngainga village for routine operational duty in preparation for the Republic Day festival. This tragic incident took place when most of the villagers had gone to Halang village to attend the conference of the Tangkhul community's apex students' body (Tangkhul Katamnao Long). The incident occurred while Luingamla's dad was assisting his friends in constructing their house. Tharawon, her younger sister, was also in the kitchen garden, cleaning the garden. All of a sudden, a loud noise was heard, followed by a woman's voice for help. Thereafter, two gunshots were heard. After that, neighbors rushed to Luingamla's house and saw her lying on the kitchen floor in a pool of overflowing blood, and her mouth was gagged with a piece of cloth. The two Indian Army officers were on the spot and Captain Mandhir Singh was cleaning the blood that was spilled on his trousers.

Seeing the neighbors coming, the two Army officers shouted that some insurgents had killed her. The two Army officers called their jawans from the post located nearby and declared a curfew. The Armed Forces forcefully gathered all the villagers inside the village playground in search of the killer. Zamthingla Ruivah, who had seen the two Army officers killing Luingamla Muinao gave a half-smile and said, "They killed her because she did not allow them to do their dirty deed. She died protecting her chastity. Yet the shipai [soldiers] were again torturing the villagers."

Protest rally cum funeral procession of Ms. Luingamla Muinao.

Source: Naga by Blood (FB) & Pei Lui

Tangkhul community reacted to the killing of Luingamla Muinao by boycotting the Indian Republic Day. Since that year, the Ngainga Shanao Long (Ngainga Women's Body) changed its foundation day to 26th January, embodying some form of remembrance of pain and protest as well as a commemoration of the death of Luingamla Muinao. But it was only after twenty-five years that the memorial column was erected and unveiled on

23rd October 2011. The epitaph on the front face of the column reads, Sacred Memorial: "Weep no more mummy, let the world know I have sacrificed my life in preserving a woman's chastity and dignity blessed by God the Creator. Lt. Miss Luingamla Muinao (Maza)." The case went on for four years but nothing much was done. However, in response to the widespread agitation against the killing, an army court-martial was conducted in 1988 and the army captain Mandhir Singh was court-martialled, but the lieutenant was acquitted and scot-free.

In order to remember Luingamla Muinao, her neighbor Zamthingla Ruivah designed a beautiful Phanek/Mekhela with a woolen garment called Luingamla Kashan. It is worn by the Tangkhul women to remember Luingamla and as a symbol of resistance on some important occasions.

Chaos and terror in Ukhrul town:

The terror attack upon innocent civilians in Ukhrul is still painful to remember. Memories of 9th May 1994 are still fresh in the minds of the Tangkhul community. On that fateful day, Major Bakshi and Asst. Commandant Labh Singh were approaching Wino Bazar (the central market of Ukhrul town) at around 5:00 p.m. from their 20 Assam Rifles town post, which is just 30 meters away. They suspected insurgents, ambushed and fired upon them. Major Bakshi was hit by a bullet and died on the spot; Asst. Comdt. Labh Singh was also badly injured and succumbed to his injuries later. Captain Singh and Lance Naik N.P. Singh were another military personnel who got injured in the same attack. Out of fear and anger, the Assam Rifles personnel started firing in the direction where they suspected the militants had escaped. The Ukhrul town Wino Bazar was devastated; people were shocked by the inhumane behavior of the Assam Rifles personnel. On that fateful day, S. Mathotla, 43 years, a petrified widow who was hiding under a bed in her tailoring shop was killed when a hail of bullets splintered her head just 500 meters away from the firing incident, and S. Sochikat, a 12-year-old boy, was killed while he was stepping out of his house to fetch water.

The Assam Rifles Officials alleged that while they were transporting the victims to Somsai Unit Headquarters, they were attacked again by the insurgents near the Phungyo Baptist Church, which damaged their vehicle and some personnel were injured. But the local people reported that there was no firing after the incident, that they were just making up stories in order to justify their ferocious actions. K. Mosses Chalai, ADC Ukhrul, and in charge Deputy Commissioner, in his letter to The Secretary (Home), Govt of Manipur, Ukhrul, acknowledged that "Incessant firing continued in Ukhrul town for half an hour and after a gap of five minutes, sporadic firing continued till around 6.30 p.m." After the violent attack, there was an immediate and aggressive response by the Assam Rifles personnel. For one and a half hours, Ukhrul town was in a pathetic situation. There was indiscriminate firing by the Assam Rifles personnel. People were dragged out of their shops and houses, beaten up mercilessly, and their goods were looted. Following the cruel and aggressive incident, there were bullet marks on all the houses in Wino Bazar area. In the Wino Bazar area, every house bears bullet marks on its tin roofs and wooden walls. Residents were helpless, and the police could do no more than 'request the Assam Rifles to cease fire.' It was challenging to intervene and stop the Assam Rifles personnel because they appeared to be acting beyond their judgment.

The Assam Rifles personnel also resorted to shelling 2-inch mortars, even though they were forbidden to use those explosives in civilian areas. The mortars ripped open the roof of the Ukhrul Higher Secondary School, the only Government Higher Secondary School in the district. The Assam Rifles personnel landed in the eighth standard classroom with fierce anger, but luckily, the students had just left for the day. Anything could have happened if they had found anyone in the class. The other mortar landed on a grazing ground and killed 83-year-old Panghom Shimray on his way back home from work. About 20 mortars exploded on that day but the Assam Rifles personnel admit that they fired only one. As evidence, the police discovered shrapnel from 10 shells near the spot where the incident occured.

That same night, houses were ruthlessly searched by the Assam Rifles personnel. Nobody was allowed to move out of their house, and the district administrators and police patrolled the area throughout the night. The civil organization made countless complaints to the civil administration, of violence, physical punishment, breaking down of doors and infrastructure, looting of houses, shops, goods and cash by the Assam Rifles personnel. T. Ashang, Development Officer, United India Insurance Co. Ltd., Ukhrul Branch, whose residence-cum-office, was 'checked' by Assam Rifles personnel, who beat and kicked him severely all over his body, including his private parts. He fell to the ground while being tortured and his left ear was badly hurt, resulting in loss of hearing. Furthermore, all his relatives who took shelter in his home were also tortured and beaten without any reason. All of them were beaten so badly that they were hospitalized the next day. Even a village elder who is an ex-army man was not spared; they observed him carefully and beat him ruthlessly without any evidence. The Assam Rifles personnel came down on the village locality intending to terrorize or seek revenge and spared nobody they met on the way. Mr. Kong Kan, a Second World War veteran, was badly tortured and beaten up after this incident.

According to the confidential communication to the Home Secretary, Imphal, the ADC also acknowledged: "Over forty are admitted to district hospital, Ukhrul. The town is under deep shock and fear and is under the apprehension of further harassment. I request you to kindly take up the matter with the highest army authorities." Another source from the ADC reflects the lack of implementation of any proper system as concerns the confinement of women by the security forces. It states: "On 9th May 1994, A.R. personnel apprehended 19 people and took them to the Somsai Camp. This includes 4 women. They were handed over to the police on the 10th of May 1994 night. On 15th May 1994, while meeting with Commander 'B' Range, 10 Sector & C.O. 20 A.R. it was pointed out that in the future it would be better to hand over the female suspects to police custody and interrogations may be done in police custody itself, and that the district Administration holds them as long as security forces desire so, needless to emphasize that confining of women in the security Forces Camps is a highly sensitive issue and causes a lot of damage against the best interests of everyone concerned, particularly for the State".

Unsurprisingly, the Assam Rifles simply refuted all the charges brought against them by taking advantage of the stand, protected by the Armed Forces Special Power Act implemented under the legislation. Thus, no further action could be taken against them even though they violated human rights. The President of the Tangkhul Naga Long, Mr. Leiyo Kazingmei of Lunghar village, summarised the role that the security forces played in the area over the last four decades. "The Army has come here to protect the people, but they harass us instead. The army has been here in Ukhrul since 1956. We have grown up with it in the center of town. In the beginning, the army was friendly, cooperative, and helpful. Today, they are fighting the civilians instead of the insurgents. There is hardly any family where someone has not been a victim of army atrocities. Every family has a sad story to tell".

About the effect of such militarization in the area on the lives of women, women leaders Veronica Zingkhai, President, Tangkhul Shanao Long, and Thokchuila Hongray noted, "Women are frightened to go anywhere near uninformed men. Let alone grown-up women, even little girls are ogled at by army personnel and they pass rude comments". Women in Ukhrul do not take the main road that passes through the Assam Rifles town post. Instead, they chose to take a long narrow roundabout rough route to avoid meeting the army personnel. "Women are the mainstay of the Naga economy", they continued, "and the presence of the army has restricted their mobility considerably. There have been cases of rape but they are not brought out into the open. There are many incidents of physical torture and killing by the army, but the fact that the army is sitting in the center of the town is the biggest mental harassment. They can go anywhere within a short time. Nowadays, even when a tyre bursts, ordinary citizens fear blank firing by the army. We have made several applications for the removal of the army post from the center of Ukhrul town but our pleas have fallen on deaf ears."

Mr. Standhope Varah, President, Tangkhul Student's Union said, "We are not against the army personnel, but we are against the policies of the Central Government, which does not want to solve the half-a-century-old 'Naga problem'. Every time the Naga nationalists create a problem, there is an overreaction from the army against the civilians. We are against that. Ultimately, what is needed is a political solution. In the '50s and '60s, the Nagas were united, but now we are fragmented. Naga nationalism is no more and tribalism has taken over, thanks to the policies of the Indian Government. They have realized that it is difficult to fight against united Naga nationalists. So, they did everything to divide the Naga people. Now they have thrown a bone among the dogs. New Delhi has proposed unconditional talks but whom will Delhi talk to? Which faction can control all the insurgents? This will be a big problem; our problem has been compounded and complicated in the last 50 years." But the fact is that the policies and approach of the State Government and Central Government played a very critical role in determining the lives of the people of Manipur.

It is the Assam Rifles and other Security personnel posted in the state that impact their lives on a daily basis. This became a threat to the overall development of the Tangkhul community. The socio-economic and living condition of the Tangkhul community is badly affected by the act of continuous violence happening in Ukhrul district.

Arson attack on Huishu village:

On 11th March 1996, some suspicious NSCN (IM) men attacked the Assam Rifles Camp at Huishu village in Ukhrul District. The heavy exchange of firing between the two groups lasted for almost three hours. The episode was a notorious one as this was the first time women were used as human shields by the armed personnel of the Government of India. A village woman named Khachungla was used as a shield to cover Captain Sharma with a Naga Shawl while going near the location where a heavy exchange of gun firing was going on between the two groups. Following the attack and the exchange of fire, the Assam Rifles set the entire village on fire. The Assam Rifles personnel torched 153 houses one by one. They ransacked all the houses and collected all the valuable materials in the sack before torching the houses. The helpless villagers stood still and watched their house burn down to ashes. What followed was the military operation in which three people were killed and many others were subjected to brutal torture.

Only the church, school building, and a few houses located in odd places were spared. No other dwelling place was spared. One hundred seven houses were reported to have been burnt down and the villagers fled to the jungle. Some of them who fled towards Poi village were fired upon by the Assam Rifles and they were forced to march back to Huishu under the command of Captain Sharma. When some groups of captured villages and the Assam Rifles personnel were coming near the village, some bullets were shot in their direction. Out of fear, the villagers tried to escape but they were not allowed to hide. Instead, they were used as human shields by the Assam Rifles personnel to protect them from bullets. In the meantime, out of fear, they fired their bullets randomly. That day, the villagers spent their night inside the church, with all the window panes damaged and the light bulbs smashed up by the angry Assam Rifles personnel. Approximately Rs. 15 lakhs were looted while raiding the houses and property of several lakhs were burnt down to ashes by the Assam Rifles who considered themselves "Friends of the Hill People".

Villagers suspect that by taking advantage of the Tangkhul Baptist Long Centenary Celebrations in Ukhrul, which were being attended by many members of the underground forces, the army had decided to raid one of the NSCN camps at the Burma border. The Huishu Assam Rifles post may have been attacked by the militant group to distract the army. Some facts about Huishu village make the trauma following the incident of March 11 all the more horrific, evoking a keen sense of sadness or regret. The nearest bus stop is almost 20 km from the village while the closest medical aid is 10 km away. The nearest source of water is at a distance of 4 km away from the village. There used to be piped water but it was all burnt down. The army post, about less than half a km away, has its own water supply. There is a government school in the village but it does not function. The hills around the village are completely bare and desolate. One wonders where the people will get the timber to rebuild their houses or the mental strength to rebuild their lives.

During this time, the NPMHR Delhi, along with other media organizations, organized All India Fact Finding Team comprising of NPHRM, NWUM (Naga Women's Union Manipur), ANSUM (All Naga Student Union of Manipur) JWP (Joint Women's Programme) Imphal, and two journalists from Imphal took up the task to look into the cases related to human rights in the state. One member of each of the teams was sent to all the districts of Manipur. This fact-finding team tried to inquire about the motive of the attack by the NSCN. When the fact-finding team met Col. L.B. Mishra, Commander Officer of Somsai, Ukhrul, he was impatient to give his version, especially about Huishu village. At the same time, he called everyone who came to inquire about this incident 'a stooge of the NSCN'.

Ms. Shirajli from Maharastra arrived at Ukhrul District for investigation. The TSL President Miss Veronica Zingkhai met Miss Shirajli and narrated the atrocities committed by the armed personnel of the state in detail. She also submitted a report along with photographs about the atrocities committed from 1974 until 1996, including the Huishu village burning incident. Apart from this, the TSL President, together with the Tangkhul Katamnao Saklong (TKS) and NPMHR, took Ms. Shirajli to Huishu Village so that she could witness firsthand what actually had happened in the village. The TSL requested the visiting team to help with the issues of the immediate repeal of the Armed Forces Special Power Act 1958 and to remove the 20th Assam Rifles post from the heart of Ukhrul.

On 2nd June 1996, the 5th Sikh Light Infantry gathered the villagers of Jessami and detained them for two consecutive days. Jessami is the last village in Ukhrul district bordering Nagaland. The village is a junction of trade between Nagaland and Manipur and many non-Tangkhuls like Chakesang, Meiteis, Nepali, and Biharis live there for business purposes. The Army has been stationed in Jessami since the 1950s. Over the years, the people of Jessami have negotiated their co-existence with both the army and the underground insurgents with their characteristic "Market- Craft".

Torture in villages:

On January 2, 1996, at about 4:00 pm, six or seven Jawans came with their vehicle to the bazaar of Jessami and after making an abrupt turn, blank-fired their bullets. A Nepali named Vicky Tamang was in a hotel owned by a Muslim family. Upon seeing the Jawans coming, he ran outside and shouted. The jawans asked him, "where is that man"? He pointed to a boy who hailed from Jessami. But out of fear, the boy started to run. The jawans fired bullets at the boy and he was shot dead. On hearing the shots of gunfire, around 15-16 jawans rushed down to the spot from their post. All of a sudden, the jawans started shooting blindly at all four corners of the bazaar, and Tamang was also hit. However, the army claimed that Tamang was shot by the NSCN militants. Tamang was interrogated by the district Superintendent of Police but he gave a false report that Tamang was not shot by the jawans. Subtly, the report was a contradictory made-up story.

Many villagers were brutally tortured and three women, including a pregnant housewife, were molested in front of their husbands. Fingers were inserted into their private parts. Some villagers were in the church when Captain Ashwin suddenly entered the church along with his jawans and headed straight for the pulpit. He pointed his pistol at the worshipers and warned them to stop worshiping and chanting prayers, or else he would shoot them. The jawans separated men and women and made them stand on either side of the church. Two visitors from Kachai village were taken by the jawans to their post and tortured brutally. The jawans brutally beat another person inside the church out of suspicion since he belonged to Talloi village. After two days, the two visitors from Kachai village were released and given into the hands of the village authority. But since they were beaten badly, one of them could not stand and walk on his own. The police wireless operator, the village school principal, the village chairman, the village secretary, and a Nepali blacksmith were tortured the most and they sustained serious injuries. All of them were beaten so badly that they had to be taken to Imphal for treatment.

The village authority of Jessami responded quickly and effectively after the incident and made a series of representations at all levels, starting with the DC of the Ukhrul district, the Chief Minister, and the Prime Minister of India. The village authority of Jessami requested to remove the 4th Sikh Light Regiment from their locality, but it was not removed despite a series of Human rights violations committed by them. Due to the various representations at high levels and because of the sensitiveness of the locality, inquiries were held. The Chairman and the Secretary were summoned to the camp and forced to sign some papers, but they refused, saying that they could not sign anything without the consent of the village committee. Therefore, they hosted a "Burra Khana" for all the village committees, where alcoholic drinks were served and everyone was forced to drink. When all of them got highly drunk, they called all of them one by one and forced them to sign a statement that they were not allowed to read and they did not even know what they were made to sign. Each one was photographed while signing and Captain Ashwini Nayyar went so far as to tell them that the army has a very good relationship with the villagers of Jessami, who are actually very innocent, and alluded that the members of the village authority had made false accusations against the army because they were 'misguided'.

On 10th July 1997, a few Northern villages of Ukhrul dist. Razai Khullen, Jessami, Wahong, New Tusom, and Soraphung villages were covered by the 4th Shik L-I and were under physical, mental, and economic harassment. Men were at risk of being harassed anywhere without any reason if they ran into the Armed Forces. In January 1997, Captain Vinod Lamba, the Post Commander, after severely beating up eight members of village authority and three students of new Tusom, compelled the Headman of that village to issue a Press release drafted by the Captain, stating that the Sikh L-I has been cooperating with the villagers and that there is a cordial relationship between the Armed forces and the civilians. The Armed Forces spread over the paddy fields and the jungle with a heavy presence of armed jawans in the field. Womenfolk could not continue their normal agricultural activities. The womenfolk were constantly accompanied by men for their protection.

The Armed Forces usually conduct house-to-house raids and grouping of villagers at their own will. In May 1996 alone they had conducted such operations twice. There are instances where vegetables and clothes are forcefully taken. The clothes which they returned were badly worn and torn. Whenever the villagers objected, they were threatened by saying, "you must supply these things to NSCN for free. Why do you refuse us?"

Tanrui village incident 22nd August 2001:

On 22nd Aug 2001 at 2:00 am column of AR under the Command of Captain Digvendra, Post Commander Kachai Post, picked up 4 innocent civilians of Tanrui village, which is situated 13 km. away from Kachai Post, Ukhrul District.

The following are the innocent civilians:

1. Phungmayang Horam (aged 25) farmer s/o Apam Hora
2. Gedeon Horam (aged 45) V.A. s/o late Horza Horam
3. VS. Jonah (aged 64) Asstt. Paster s/o late VS. Yarteo and
4. LK. John (aged 42) V.A s/o LK Harkhon, all from Kachai Village.

They were blindfolded and dragged into the deep jungle beyond the boundary of Tanrui village and tortured inhumanely, forced to locate NSCN Camp, intimidated to be shot dead if they failed to locate NSCN Camp, and resorted to many rounds of blank fire. Some of the victims of the incident are on the verge of losing their eyesight due to incessant punching and kicking.

To rescue the victims from the brutality of Assam Rifles, the womenfolk of the Tanrui Village shouldered the risk of following them up to the deep jungle. On their way, one Major of Assam Rifles came into contact in the Jungle of Sirarakhong, which is around 20 km. away from Tanrui village (victims' village), and helped them by identifying the directions in which the victims were taken away by Captain Digvendra.

When the womenfolk reached the place where the victims were detained, Captain Digvendra apologized and begged for forgiveness by offering Rs.

100/- each to the victims but they refused his offer. After a few days, Kachai Post Commander sent one Subedar to clarify that the incident had happened due to wrong information that they received from their informer.

They tried to console the villagers by giving assurance that AR is ready to extend any help or assistance if the villagers would approach them. The villager gave a clear message to the AR that they were not happy with what the AR had done during Ceasefire so they would not ask for any help from AR.

The AR Kachai Post issued a press statement on the incident through IFP saying that the AR had busted an abundant NSCN Camp in the jungle of Tanrui village without mentioning anything done to the innocent villagers.

Shot to death:

RW. Silas aged 30 s/o RW. Machihan of Khayang village, Ukhrul District was shot dead by Assam Rifles personnel inside the bus in which the victim was traveling to Shangkai under Litan Police Station on the fateful day of 12th August 1993. On the same day, a woman from Sharkaphung village died due to the random shelling of two mortars by the Assam Rifles personnel.

17th August 1994 Incident:

On 17th August 1994, a column of AR personnel were coming to Ukhrul. On reaching Ukhrul the Army personnel suddenly opened fire without any provocation and it continued for about one hour. One of the bullets ribbed through the wooden plank of a house and fatally wounded Ms. H. Wonchungla, 14 years old, a student of Pakshimi High School Ukhrul, who was in her study room. She was rushed to the District Hospital, Ukhrul, but declared dead within half an hour at about 8.00 pm.

The same group of 20 AR, while passing through Viewland, shot another person named Mr. Mahai about 30 years old, a butcher by profession. He was a lefty but to frame him as an Under Ground (UG) activist, the Assam Rifles personnel left an unserviceable pistol on the right hand of the victim.

House raid and arbitrary arrest:

Sporadic midnight raids were conducted by the 20th Assam Rifles. Hotels and private houses were terrorized on 12th May 1997. The doors of the hotels and houses they raided were rudely kicked open and the inmates were forced to kneel down while they ransacked and searched the houses. Essential household items were robbed and even bedclothes were not spared. At some houses, the male members were beaten while women and children shrieked in anger and fear. In other places, many were forcefully taken away. Among the arrests, one particular incident was recorded at Greenland, Ukhrul. Mr. Masoyang Singnaisui and his brother were picked up from their house. Having found no fault with them, the Assam Rifles personnel accused them of keeping 30 kgs of Ganja in large quantity, which they had kept. This entire raid took place from 11:00 am to 2:30 am. Having terrorized and robbed people's peace and privacy, the Assam Rifles personnel forced every householder to sign statements denying any damage, destruction, and harm by the raid and the midnight raids continued for four consecutive nights.

On May 13, 1997, in Wino Bazar, Ukhrul, Mr. Somi Shaiza's residence was raided, during which Rs. 15,000/- in cash was stolen from the householder. Mr. Somi Shaiza was subsequently arrested at around 1:00 am.

On 6th June 1997, two young boys, Mr. Wungnaoyo and Mr. Mashunthing, both from Shimtang village, Ukhrul District, about 20-22 years of age, sand and gravel dealers by profession, were picked from Hotel Eastern Mount, Phungreitang, Ukhrul, adjacent to Viewland at about 1:30 to 2:00 pm. According to fellow boarders who eye-witnessed the raid and arrest, the raiding AR personnel had started beating the two boys right in front of the Hotel. On the same night, two more people were reported to have been picked by the AR personnel from Greenland locality of Ukhrul. Two more boys at Winow Bazar and another boy from Viewland Bazar were picked up in broad daylight at around 1: 00 pm as filed by the public who witnessed the incident. Their whereabouts were still unknown till the filing of the report at 6:00 pm.

In the wake of such inhuman acts, the Tangkhul Katamnao Long organized a peace rally on the streets of Ukhrul town. All the schools, colleges, students, and various Civil Society Organizations (CSOs) participated in the rally.

In another regretful incident in the early hours, at about 3:15 am on 9th July 1997, the Army operation in Ukhrul town raided the dwelling home of Mr. A.S. Katuishang of Phungreitang (House no. B-362). The householder and wife were taken away to the paddy fields. The house was left under the care of Mr. A.S Katuishang's sister-in-law. According to the caretaker woman, she was forced to open the door and almirah. Then she was kept at gunpoint while some jawans started searching every article they could lay their hands on. The poor caretaker woman did not know what had been done to the household. After the jawans left, she found that Rs.1000 was missing from her purse, which was lying empty. And when Ms. Angela, the lady of the house, returned home in the afternoon she found that Rs 5,300 had been robbed by the jawans. In fact, she had kept the money in a safe place.

The house lady promptly reported the incident to the district Deputy Commissioner, Superintendent of Police, and Tangkhul Naga Long for the immediate retrieval of the stolen amount.

On 18th November 2000 Mr. Mark Ramsan, aged 46, Chowkidar of District Co-operative Ukhrul, was arrested along with his wife Ms. Zingkumwon, aged 26, from his quarter at 1:00 am on the charge that the victims were found keeping Rs. 25,000 in cash. The victims have saved the money for their future security but the outrageous Assam Rifle returned only Rs. 24,000.

Arrest of CEO on the 10th April 1997:

The residence of Mr. Ramdhar, Chief Executive Officer (CEO), Ukhrul Autonomous District Council, at Bumrei, Hundung, within a radius of 1 km. from Ukhrul DC Office, was raided at 11:00 pm. by the 20th AR of Ukhrul. The raiding party ransacked almost everything in the house. Mr.

K. Ramdhar, Class I Officer, was blindfolded and taken away to an unknown destination. According to Mr. K. Ramdhar, he was tied and slapped in the face several times. He could not make out where he was. The next day, at about 4.30 am, he was dropped at Jessami Junction, Viewland, Ukhrul, where his blindfold was removed. He said that he was forced to sign a statement denying any harassment or torture at the place where he was beaten.

Midnight raid at Kamphasom tang:

The 20th AR Jawans raided Mr. A.S. Kumar's house at Kamphasom at around 2:30 am on 11th June 1997. According to student boarders, the doors were rudely kicked open and every nook and corner was searched, even bedclothes and boxes.

On 11th June 1997, Mr. Y. Ngathinghor, aged about 25 years and a married man, was picked from Viewland Bazar, Ukhrul at noon when he was buying essential items. The AR personnel picked him up along with the groceries he was holding in a polythene bag, said those who eye-witnessed the incident. He had not returned home till 5:30 pm therefore the report was filed.

Mr. AS. Shimreiyo, vice President of TNL, was raided at his home at Kamphasom, Phungraitang, Ukhrul, by the AR Jawans accompanied by a masked man at 11:30 pm. When the President of the whole Tangkhul Naga Community stood at gunpoint, the masked man physically assaulted him by slapping and punching his face in front of his wife and children.

That same night, the General Secretary of the TNL was pulled out and dragged up to the main road where he was forced to kneel on the bare hard surface.

The civilian population of Ukhrul imposed a 12-hour bandh on 14th June 1997 in condemnation of excesses committed by the AR. The district people Joint Action Committee served a Memorandum to Shri O.N. Srivastava, terming the army actions as an "Extra-constitutional military Showdown", and calling for immediate intervention of the Governor.

Indeed, the unarmed and innocent civil population of Ukhrul had to wait helplessly for the day of peace and respect for human rights to come, which may or may not come as early as they desired.

Brutal Beating of Sports Officers:

In an unfortunate case of Human Rights Violation on 10th Dec. 1999 by Bn. M.R. Personnel, wherein five innocent public leaders and officers of Ukhrul District Sports Association (UDSA), Sports Authority of India (SAI), and Sports Department were brutally beaten and one of the victims received bullet injury without any sufficient cause.

The incident happened as they were proceeding towards Youth Hostel, Ukhrul, to drop off the coaches of SAI and groceries like eggs, bananas, apples, etc. for the SAI players who were stationed at Youth Hostel, Ukhrul. On reaching the gate, which is on the premises of the Youth & Sports Department complex, the sentry of the 6th Bn. Manipur Rifles urged- "Open the gate yourself to enter". Compelled to follow the order, Mrs. Phaningmi removed the stone which was blocking the gate. With the opening of the gate, almost half of their vehicles drove inside the gate. At that very moment, two 6th Bn. M.R. personnel in civilian dress came in running and refused to let them enter. To convene, M.R. personnel Mr. L Maya Junior Youth Officer Sports Department, identified himself and being an officer of sports department, he asserted his right to enter the Youth Hostel/own office and also made it clear to M.R. personnel that all the occupants in the vehicle are public leaders and officers of UDSA, SAI & Sports Department. But contrarily, all pleas fell on deaf ears, and the M.R. personnel in plain civilian clothes started physically assaulting Mr. S. Phaningmi.

To intervene in the situation, the occupants of the vehicles got down at once. On seeing this movement, one of the M.R personnel in plain clothes ran towards the sentry post and after taking the sentry's service rifles, fired two rounds in the air. Then many M.R. personnel, including Mr. James Manao Sasa Asst. Comdt. of 6th Bn.M.R. came out, followed by a rain of blow of rifles' butts, clubs, and boots. After beating up the victims blue and black, some rounds were fired, which resulted in a bullet injury to the thigh of Mr. Yaopam, an officer of UDSA. Even though this was

M.R. personnel's inhuman, uncultured act, the victims were charged with "Illegal trespassing and attempting to snatch arms, which virtually amounts to a "Criminal case" against the innocent public leaders and officers of UDSA, SAI & Sports Dept." The victims struggled to survive due to severe injuries inflicted on them and had to be hospitalized to save their lives.

Curfew imposed on Villagers:

At Talui junction, conducting body searches of passengers, travelers, and pedestrians at random points started in February 2000 after a lull of more than two years from the date of the Indo-Naga ceasefire effect. Apart from the regular checkpoints, random checking and frisking were carried out at Talui junction, Choithar-Khangkhui junction, and midway between Ukhrul and Finch-Corner. Buses and other vehicles were frequently detained for hours after searches and checking, causing immense discomfort and economic loss to innocent passengers and travelers. Even transportation of daily needs like firewood was restricted.

In another incident without the knowledge of the District Magistrate Assam Rifles took the law into their own hands and imposed a curfew for five consecutive days upon a cluster of villages namely: Talui, Theiva, Kachai, Ngari, Khongtei, and Tingshong from 7th to 12th of August 2000, which forced the public to cease from daily activities like venturing to paddy fields, attending schools, offices, and it even restricted them from carrying medicines and any essential items. Hoomi-bound passenger bus (daily service) came to a standstill as many travelers were stranded at several junctions. They were randomly firing at night and blasting bombs such as 2-inch motors in the wilderness, obviously to frighten the innocent population and intimidate them, like demanding that they hand over the corpses hidden in their village and that anyone seen outside their home at odd hours would be shot down by the officers of the Armed Forces and the Deputy Inspector General of Police (DIG) himself. The Armed Forces also arbitrarily collect rice and vegetables from the villagers. Such activities generated fear in the minds of the villagers. In the course of the Assam Rifles' operation, many people were called for interrogation, intimidated, and detained for days, including government servants and minors on the charges of carrying medicines at the time of checking by the Assam Rifles personnel.

Some of the arrested victims were (i) Ms. Ramyophi (12) a student of class VI (ii) Ms. K. Tammila (14) class VIII, (iii) K. Nimmisho (14) class VI, (iv) Ms. K. Worngamla (12) class VI, (v) Mr. CL. Khayuingam (21)

B.E. (vi) Mr. K. Tharmasing (50), Teacher, (vii) Mr. CL. Tuimi (22) Class XII, (viii) Mr. HL. Luimavai (23) Pharmacist, (ix) Mr. S. Thotmathing (29) Teacher and others were arrested at Talui Junction by the 20 Assam Rifles personnel when the arrestees were traveling to Talui by a jeep. Among the nine people arrested, six were women Integrated Child Development Services (ICDS) Scheme workers on their way to deliver medicines to Anganwadi Centres under United Nations International Children's Emergency Fund (UNICEF) programs namely:

(1) Ms. R. Ramhorla, aged 35 w/o R. Sharei,

(2) Ms. R. Khayila, aged 35 d/o R. Tarei

(3) Ms. V. Ningchimla, aged 45 d/o V. Wungchan

(4) Ms. RS. Lily, aged 40 d/o RS. Moreiphung

(5) Ms. V. Hildah, aged 39 w/o V. Khavangkhut

All ICDS employees belong to Talui village and the other three are identified as:

(1) Mr. RK. Luithing, aged 28 s/o Late RK. Lungthuk, Driver

(2) Mr. L. Yuingrei, aged 20 s/o L. Wungnaosui, student

(3) Mr. RK. Pamching, aged 50 s/o RK. Kharim, Permanent Cooli of the Public Works Department, Govt. of Manipur

There was no charge against any of them in the release paper issued by the Police Station at Ukhrul. However, nine innocent people were detained at the 20 AR, Ukhrul Town Post for over 23 hours. Mrs. Masophi Nakhadei, age 54, child Development Project Officer, ICDS was rudely awakened at 11.00 pm. from her sleep by the Assam Rifles personnel and was taken to their post to identify the arrested ICDS employees mentioned above. She was detained there till 1.00 a.m. on 8th August 2000.

To enforce the law of the land to mitigate the grievances of the innocent public, NPMHR Ukhrul called upon District Magistrate Ukhrul and immediately sent a team headed by Sub-Divisional Magistrate to the affected area. It was reported that the SDM Team could not proceed further than Talui on the same day due to prolonged detention at two checkpoints on their way by Assam Rifles personnel. At Talui Post, AR Official advised them not to proceed beyond Talui for security reasons, stating that "Hundred of Assam Rifles' personnel were deployed in that region and as such, the AR personnel could fire upon them on mistaken identity." On receiving the report of the SDM, NPMHR Ukhrul volunteered to visit the affected area to assess the situation on the spot with an understanding of the District Magistrate to station a Magistrate to enforce the Rule of Law in the affected area till normalcy was restored.

Indiscriminate firing:

On 18th Nov. 2000 at 1: 00 am under the command of Captain Mr. Satarji, Assam Rifles resorted to indiscriminate firing in the civil populated place at Phungreitang Ukhrul without any reason. The flying bullets ribbed through the kitchen of Mr. Athing Shimray aged 43 S/o S Shangam of Khangkhui Village, damaging a Gas Cylinder, Washing Machine Basin, and a Chinese Cup.

After some minutes of gunshots, around 10 to 15 Assam Rifle personnel led by a Subedar came and interrogated the house owner, who fired those shots? The Assam Rifle personnel checked all the rooms. For the second time, a team led by Assam Rifle Captain came in while the house owner was trying to close the door, which was opened by the Assam Rifle while checking the house. The Captain shouted, "where are you trying to run away? Open all the doors, etc." They stayed there till morning and left after picking up all the remains of the bullet shots. They tried to console the house owner that all the damages caused by the gunshots would be compensated.

The house owner reported the incident to the Deputy Commissioner/District Magistrate of Ukhrul, begging for mitigation of the grievances. But the District Magistrate, contrary to the expectation of the applicant, warned the victims to refrain from keeping a close relationship with the NSCN cadre. Thus, the whole story of the unfortunate case of Human Rights Violation was forced to remain hidden in the hearts of the helpless victims.

The ambush on the 21st Sikh Regiment by NSCN (IM) at Namthilok between Imphal and Ukhrul on 19th Feb. 1982 resulted in the killing of 21 soldiers, including the Major of the 21st Sikh Regiment. The reason for the attack was the inhuman notoriety of sodomy committed by the Armed forces. After the ambush, the District Magistrate Gyan Prakash Joshi declared a collective fine of Rs.100 per household on three villages, Sikibung, Shangkai, and Lamlai Chingphei, which were lying near the ambush spot. The villagers were herded to the road like animals, tortured badly, and roughly interrogated by the soldiers. The District Magistrate ordered the deadline for the payment of the fine by July 31st, but District Magistrate Gyan Prakash Joshi and district police personnel forcibly collected fines from these three villages three days before the deadline. The district police personnel forcibly pulled out the properties and restored them only when the fine was fully paid up. It was a shocking experience for the villagers as the District Magistrate and district police personnel were rather involved in such an inhuman act of violation instead of giving protection.[30]

Incident of Sodomy:

On 6th March 1982, Mr. Z. Kuileng (15) of Phungcham village was detained by two 21st Sikh Regiment jawans while he was going to Ukhrul from his

---

[30] Yambem Laba, "The statement: Tale of two ambushes,"

village Phungcham to get new trousers from the tailor. They asked him whether he knew a Naga Army which he denied. They asked him if he knew any girl outside his village, and he replied he didn't. Then one of the jawans tied his hands and took him into the jungle, where the jawan committed sodomy. He had to undergo for medical examination the following day at Ukhrul Hospital.[31]

Recording of the negotiation between 20 AR Ukhrul and Ngariching Living Centre, Viewland, Ukhrul in the Office of the Naga Peoples' Movement Human Rights, Ukhrul on 10-02-2002.

Members present: 13 (thirteen), Recorded by: Chansa Luithui

The meeting was held to solve mutually in good faith, the incident that happened on 8th February 2002 at Ngariching Living Centre (NLC) Viewland, Ukhrul, in which Mr. Ganesh, Hav. 20 AR of Somsai Ukhrul allegedly attempted to sodomise a differently-abled (totally blind) inmate of NLC after forcibly getting him drunk. Maj. Yogesh Chaudhury Ukhrul Town Post Commander represented 20 AR Mr. T. Huimi Guardian of NLC, Mr. Ahao, owner of the building, and a member of NPMHR, Ukhrul.

On behalf of the 20 AR Somsai Ukhrul Maj. Yogesh Chaudhury outrightly condemned the uncultured act committed by G.K. Singh Havildar, E-Coy. 20 AR and it was concluded that the culprit shall apologize in front of all the members present, to prove the sincerity of the principle "mutually in good faith" apart from necessary disciplinary action under the Army Act. It was also agreed that the action taken against the culprit shall be communicated to all the parties concerned.

The culprit, Mr. G.K. Singh, Hav. 20 AR was immediately summoned to the NPMHR Office. He came and confessed that he had committed his act of misbehavior towards the handicapped inmate of NLC in front of everyone present. In return, the FIR lodged in the Ukhrul police station was withdrawn forthwith to facilitate the transfer of the issue to the Commandant of 20 AR Ukhrul, for necessary action under Army Act as agreed upon.

Having the assurance given in front of the parties concerned, an application to affect the withdrawal of the FIR lodged in the Ukhrul Police was signed

---

[31] Shimreingam A Shishak (2016) The Nagas: Yesterday, today & tomorrow, part-1 Chapter-1&2, yesterday & today

by the petitioner Mrs. T. Hormila and the complaint was lodged with the Commandant 20 AR Ukhrul.

Before the dispersal, Col. Rajkumar Commandant 20 AR appeared on the scene, to whose command the culprit belonged. He appreciated that the process worked out and assured that necessary action would be taken. Having thus changed the process in confidence, the negotiation came to an end.

Recordings of Human Rights Violation Incidents Specific to Ukhrul District From 1st August to 25th September 2000. NPMHR, Ukhrul

Despite Nagas' Open Boycott of the last two parliamentary elections (to the 12th and 13th), there was total peace in the district. Since 1st August 1997, the day the Indo-Naga Ceasefire was put into effect, no bullet was heard from the barrels of the armed forces on both sides. The threat to the prevailing peace first emerged when the state assembly elections were about to take place in February 2000. The Armed Forces of the government of India intensified security measures, conducting frisks not only at regular checkpoints but also establishing new checkpoints at random. The first gunshot since the declaration of Indo-Naga Ceasefire was fired by the CRPF on election duties at the counting center of the district. The curfew under Section 144 of the Criminal Procedure Code (CrPC) was relaxed in the counting area, specifically at the Ukhrul Town Hall, with restrictions limited to a certain square meterage. This led to the closure of approximately 85 shops and workshops within the Section 144 CrPC designated area, reigniting Human Rights concerns in the district.

I. **Frisking and sporadic house raids:**

Sporadic house raids were conducted by the AR personnel at night and as well as during the daytime at Wino Bazar, Viewland, Phungreitang, and the 7th Finance Quarters. No arrest could be made but fear was generated and inconveniences were caused to the residents of those houses.

II. **Arrest and brutal torture of Mr. K. Chihanpam:**

Mr. K. Chihanpam, a 60-year-old, son of late K. Pamphaleng and a resident of Kamjong, was apprehended from a vehicle at Gamnum by the 25th Assam Rifles (AR) personnel manning the Gamnum Camp on August 26, 2000. He was taken into custody after explosive materials were discovered in his bag. Subsequently, he was blindfolded, and the AR troops began physically assaulting him.

III. Threat letter to the churches:

An unofficial circular without an address to and from was served to all churches in Ukhrul and surrounding villages on the 3rd of September 2000 by Assam Rifles' Jawans in full uniform from the 20th AR Ukhrul. The full context of the circular goes as under:

NSCN (IM) is responsible for disturbing peace and tranquility in the region and they were planning to strike in Ukhrul District. It has already carried out strikes against Security Forces in various parts of Manipur, including Senapati and Tamenglong districts, and now it is planning strikes in Ukhrul district. The evidence of this is the recovery of a large number of explosives and bombs in Chassad, Gamnom, and Ukhrul. Because of this, the Security Force was forced to carry out searches and checks, which was against its wishes and desires. In this situation, you, the innocent people, will face hardships, difficulties, and harassment for something for which you are not responsible at all. The situation that has been created against your desire and also against the desire of the Security Force was solely due to the NSCN (IM) continuing its strike against the Security Force on the pretext of bringing peace to the region. Therefore, it is in your interest to convey to the NSCN (IM) to refrain from any such activity of an ambush or IED attack on Security Force because if it happens, then we will react very violently, which will result in damage to the public property and even loss of life. It is for you people to rise to the occasion and impress upon your misguided brothers for good sense to prevail.

IV. Isolated combing operation:

On September 21st and 22nd, 2000, a combined force of the 20th Assam Rifles (AR), Ukhrul, and the 25th AR, Shangshak, surrounded the two villages of Khangkhui Khunou and Khangkhui Khullen at night. Before dawn, the Armed Forces conducted house searches, preventing the villagers from going outside for their normal activities. On the 22nd of September, the Armed Forces did not allow the villagers to attend the mass prayer program that was scheduled to be held in the church. At Khangkhui Khunou, the Armed Forces kept the women separate from men when searches were carried out. Thus villagers were detained and robbed of the whole two 2 days' work without any cause.

V. Civil Administration response:

The District Magistrate could not do anything to safeguard the rights of the people in this district in all the major incidents of human rights violation.

NPMHR, Ukhrul Unit Comments:

Unfortunately, the state Chief Minister is a Meitei, the major community well known for his anti-Naga stand, the Deputy Commissioner, Mr. A. Ibocha Singh and the S.P. Ukhrul Mr. M. Shanti Kumar both belong to the Meitei community, so there is very little hope that the public could expect from the state Govt. and the district administration at a time like this. It has been a recurring experience of the helpless public that they are more exposed to insecurity in the security system provided by alien nationals with powers and immunity in their hands. Peace in Naga's ancestral land is being opposed by the Chief Minister of the state and no one knows what type of situation will turn in the near future.

Despite the ceasefire between GoI and NSCN (IM) it created a conducive atmosphere for bringing a lasting political solution which was in force since 1st August 1997. Numerous human rights violations continue to take place despite promising assurance to safeguard the rights of the citizens by GoI and many Dignitaries of Security Forces. In this context, the NPMHR Ukhrul Unit observing the objections raised by various Human Rights Organisations, particularly from Manipur for the extension of Ceasefire to all the Naga inhabited areas is quite surprising as this bears no justified approach, rather it clearly exhibits irrational support to perpetuate Black Laws to annihilate innocent people, which will ultimately broaden the gap between India and Naga people.

Illegal Occupation of Villages:

On 15th September 2022, more than 5000 protestors took to the streets in Ukhrul town demanding for immediate withdrawal of the Armed forces who occupied nine Tangkhul villages without their consent. The Armed forces have set up their military camps without the consensus of the villagers as their villages have been turned into veritable military garrisons.

The protest rally was organized by the Tangkhul Civil Society Organisations (CSOs) of the Tangkhul community against the forceful occupation of the villages and also for the removal of the Armed Forces (Special Powers) Act, 1958.

Knowing about the state of affairs FACAM (Forum Against Corporatization and Militarization) strongly condemned the move of the Indian State to militarily occupy Naga Villages. FACAM also alleged that the Indian state has been mocking its own constitution by constantly violating Article 371 (A) of the constitution, through such intrusions, land grabs, and Atrocities of the past and the present and granting them impunity under draconian laws like Armed Forces Special Powers Act.[32]

Picture of protest march Photo Credit: Somipei Tinphei

Memorandum was sent by CSOs to the PM through Manipur Chief Minister N Biren Singh and the same copy was forwarded to Francisco Cali Tzay

---

[32] https://nenow.in/north-east-news/manipur/manipur-villagers-stage-massive-protest-in-ukhrul-against-assam-rifles-demand-afspa-repeal.html

(UN Special Rapporteur on the Rights of Indigenous Peoples) and Gam A. Shimray (Secretary General, Asia Indigenous Peoples Pact.)

The excerpt of the memorandum reads:[33]

The Tangkhul Civil Organisations collective, as the representatives of the Tangkhul community in Manipur, wishes to place our pressing concerns with faith in your authority and leadership.

That, since 2016, an unwarranted occupation of the land by the Assam Rifles began in Chatric Khunou village. Since then, eight more villages have been occupied as outposts in the same forceful manner in the face of strong objections from the local populace in the following nine (09) villages:

1) Chatric Khunou

2) Ramphoi

3) Kangpat Khullen

4) Tusom CV

5) Poi

6) Mapum

7) Lamlang Gate

8) Khamasom Wallely

9) Kasom Khullen

The aforementioned nine military-occupied villages have been turned into veritable military garrisons. It is indeed an ungainly sight to find fully armed and combat-ready soldiers moving around in these serene villages, indicating a warlike situation when there is none and conveying the presence of hostilities when there is peace.

Therefore, with complete faith in the Prime Minister's goodwill, his undoubted love, and sense of duty toward the people, we the undersigned

---

[33] https://thefrontiermanipur.com/thousands-attend-rally-against-afspa-forceful-occupation-of-tangkhul-lands-by-assam-rifles/

herein, on behalf of the Tangkhul Naga community, are hereby obliged to make this crucial appeal to ensure the following redressal as hereunder:

1. Immediate withdrawal of the forceful Assam Rifles occupations from nine Tangkhul villages in Manipur.

Withdrawal of the Armed Forces (Special Powers) Act, 1958 (AFSPA) from all the Hill Areas/Districts of Manipur.

The memorandum further stated that many generations have been crippled in the Naga homeland under the Indian AFSPA, 1958 and a relentless effort was made from every quarter to usher peace and in light of the subsisting Ceasefire Agreement dated July 25, 1997, and the Indo- Naga Framework Agreement, dated August 3, 2015, signed between the Government of India and the National Socialist Council of Nagalim (NSCN-IM).[34]

According to the CSOs, public spaces such as schools, playgrounds, community halls, and children's homes are forcefully occupied and being used as camps by the Assam Rifles, thereby hampering their usual functioning. Moreover, security checkposts have been set up, and locals are being subjected to scrutiny as they go about their lives. In the meantime, those nine occupied villagers also staged a sit-in-protest in their villages simultaneously.[35]

---

[34] http://e-pao.net/GP.asp?src=23..160922.sep22
[35] https://www.eastmojo.com/manipur/2022/09/15/thousands-protest-in-ukhrul-against-assam-rifles-demand-afspa-repeal/

Picture of the protest rally, (Photo Credit: Somipei Tinphei)

14

INCIDENTS OF ATTACK/ AMBUSH IN UKHRUL DISTRICT, 2007 - 2017

*Data for 2007 till June 30, 2017[36]

Sl. No.	Date & Year	Place/District	Outfit	Killed	Injured
1	June 30/ 2017	Ramva, Ukhrul	PLA & MNPF	1	2
2	June 15/2017	Ukhrul	NSCN(IM)	2	Nil
3	June 15/2017	Kashung, Ukhrul	Unspecified	1	3
4	Mar 07/ 2017	Ukhrul	Unspecified	Nil	2
5	Jan 04/2017	Khunthak village	Unspecified	1	1
6	March 31/2016	Ukhrul	PLA	3	1
7	Feb 15/ 2016	Hundung Junction	PLA	Nil	Nil
8	Jan 05/ 2016	Grihang and Kamjong,	Assam Rifles	2	Nil
9	Oct 26/ 2015	Khuikai and Sampui Lamkhai	PLA	2	5
10	Oct 20/2014	Ukhrul	UNLF	3	Nil

[36] https://www.satp.org/satporgtp/countries/india/states/manipur/data_sheets/majorincidents.htm

11	Oct 08/2014	Muirei village	Unspecified	1	2
12	Sept 17/2014	Viewland, Ukhrul	Unspecified	2	Nil
13	Sept 9/2014	Ukhrul - Imphal road	Unspecified	1	2
14	Aug 30/2014	Ukhrul Town	Manipur Police	2	15
15	July 12/2014	Finch Corner	Unspecified	1	2
16	Oct 20/ 2013	Kangpat village, Ukhrul	PLA	3	5
17	September 4/ 2013	Ukhrul town	Unspecified	Nil	Nil
18	June 03/ 2013	Ukhrul Police Station,	Unspecified	Nil	Nil
19	December 28, 2012	Kongkan village	UNLF	2	Nil
20	June 30/2012	Phaikok village /Ukhrul District	KNA-Lungam	4	Nil
21	May 9/2012	Chadong Tangkhul village/Ukhrul District	PREPAK	3	Nil
22	January 26/2012	Taretlok / bordering Thoubal and Ukhrul District	CorCom	5	Nil
23	April 15/2011	Near village Riha, Ukhrul District	NSCN(IM)	8	6

24	February 11/2010	Nambasi Ukhrul	Unspecified	3	Nil
25	September 7/2009	Mokot Chepu, Ukhrul	KLA	4	Nil
26	August 12/2009	Ukhrul	NSCN(IM)	3	Nil
27	April 14/ 2009	Leishang between Kongkan villages, Ukhrul	MPA(UNLF)	1	6
28	November 26/2008	Nongdam Tangkhul, Imphal East, Senapati and Ukhrul	Unspecified	5	Nil
29	September 3/2007	Tangkhul Hundung Khunou, Ukhrul	NSCN(IM)	12	Nil
30	June 1/2007	Manturam, Ukhrul	KYKL	3	Nil
31	February 9/2007	Ukhrul	UNLF	5	1

15

IMPACT OF ARMED FORCES SPECIAL POWER ACT (AFSPA)

In this, the reasons, purposes, intensities, and severity of the Armed Forces and the human rights violation in Ukhrul district are explained accordingly.

Gender and Age of the respondents

Gender and Age are important factors for studying the scenario of human rights violations. As age increases, more experience is counted, and the level of maturity and understanding also varies accordingly. The distribution of the respondents on the basis of Gender and Age has been presented in Table No. 1.

Table no. 1

Distribution of the Gender and Age of the Respondents.

Gender	Age			Total
	between 18-40	between 41-60	61 and above	
Male	124	117	35	276
	44.9%	42.4%	12.7%	100.0%
Female	76	36	3	115
	66.1%	31.3%	2.6%	100.0%
Total	200	153	38	391
	51.2%	39.1%	9.7%	100.0%

Comparison between Gender and Age:

As per the table, out of the total 391 respondents, 115 respondents are female and 66.1% of the respondents are between the age group of *18-40*, 31.3% of the respondents are between the ages of *41-60*, and 2.6% of the respondents are at the age of 61 and above. The remaining 276 respondents are male, of which 44.9% of the respondents are between the age group of *18-40*, 42.4% of the respondents are between the age group of *41-60*, and 12.7% of the respondents are the age of 61 and above.

It was found that 51.2% of the respondents are between the age group of 18-40, 39.1% of the respondents are between the age group of 41-60, and 9.7% of the respondents are in the age of 61 and above.

Table no. 2

Information about the Agents responsible for violation of human rights.

Responsible Agents	No. of Respondents	Percent
Central Armed Forces	117	29.9
Unspecified/Unidentified	121	30.9
State police Commando and others	153	39.1
Total	391	100.0

The above table clearly indicates that out of 391 respondents, 39.1% of Human rights violations are committed by the State Police Commando and Others [Indian Reserve Battalion (IRB) and Manipur Rifles (MR) and Village Volunteer Force (VVF)], 30.9% are committed by Unidentified people and 29.9 % are committed by Central Armed Forces. It was found that State Police Commando and others committed maximum Human rights violations with 39.1%.

Thus, it can be concluded that the State Police Commando and others are the major perpetrators of Human Rights violations in Manipur state, followed by Unidentified people and Central Armed Forces.

Table no. 3

Information about the reason and purpose for Violation of Human Rights.

Reason for Violation	No. of Respondents	Percent
Out of anger	57	14.6
Due to AFSPA	129	33.0
Exposing power	199	50.9
Enmity	6	1.5
Total	391	100.0

The above table clearly indicates that out of 391 respondents, 50.9% of respondents stated that the reason and purpose for Human rights violation is due to Exposing power and only 1.5% of respondents stated their reason due to Enmity. It is observed that 33.3% responded that the reason and purpose for Human rights violation is due to the imposition of AFSPA.

Therefore, it can be concluded that the main reason for Human rights violations is the exposure of power and the imposition of AFSPA.

Table no. 4

Information about the type of rights violated.

Type of Rights violated	No. of Respondents	Percent
Right to safety and security	124	31.7
Right to protest and to gather public opinion	89	22.8
Right to autonomy and self-rule	107	27.4
Right to self-respect	66	16.9
Others	5	1.3
Total	391	100.0

The table clearly indicates that out of 391 respondents, 31.7% responded that their Right to safety and security was violated, 27.4% responded that it was a violation of Right to autonomy and self-rule and only 1.3% responded to the violation of other types of rights.

Therefore, it can be concluded that most of the respondents experienced a violation of their Right to safety and security as well as their Right to autonomy and self-rule.

Table no. 5

Information about the Crime committed by the Human Rights Violators.

Types of Crime Committed	No. of Respondents	Percent
Rape	42	10.7
Abuse	182	46.5
Murder	109	27.9
Physical abuse	56	14.3
Others	2	0.5
Total	391	100.0

The above table clearly indicates that out of 391 respondents, 46.5% of the respondents responded that the most common crime committed by Human rights violators was abuse, followed by murder 27.9%. Only 0.5% responded to other types of crimes committed by Human rights violators.

Hence, it can be concluded that the majority of the respondents believed that the most common crime committed by human rights violators was abuse, followed by murder, and physical abuse.

Table no. 6

Information about the type of punishment given by the Human Rights Violators.

Type of Punishment given	No. of Respondents	Percent
Electric shock	64	16.4
Punching and Kicking	71	18.2
Hitting with gun (Buttstroke)	106	27.1
Beating with stick (Flogging)	148	37.9
Others	2	0.5
Total	391	100.0

The above table clearly indicates that out of 391 respondents, 37.9 % responded that flogging was the most common type of punishment given by Human rights violators, followed by 27.1% which is buttstroke. Only 0.5% responded to other types of punishment.

Hence, it can be concluded that flogging and buttstroke are the most common types of punishments given by Human Rights violators.

Table no. 7

Information about the Methods of Human Rights Violation.

Methods of violation	No. of Respondents	Percent
Guns	196	50.1
Explosives	34	8.7
Physical strength	61	15.6
Teargas	99	25.3
Others	1	0.3
Total	391	100.0

The table clearly indicates that out of 391 respondents, 50.1% responded that Human rights violators used guns for committing violations, followed by the use of tear gas, which is 25.3%. Only 0.3% responded that the Human rights violators used other types of material for committing human rights violations.

Hence, it can be concluded that the most commonly used material for committing human rights violations is guns, followed by the use of tear gas.

Figure no. 8

Information about the awareness of Human Rights Law.

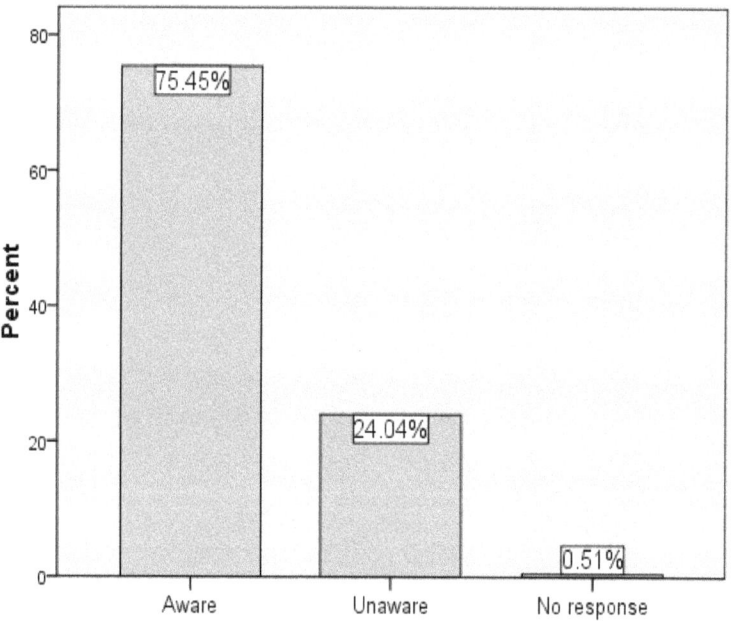

Awareness about Human Rights Law

The above Bar chart clearly indicates that out of 391 respondents, 75.45% responded that they are aware of Human rights law, and 24.04% of respondents stated that they are not aware of Human rights law. The rest 0.51% of respondents did not give any opinion about the awareness of Human rights law.

Therefore, it can be concluded that the majority of the respondents are aware of Human rights law.

Table no. 9

Information about the State government and the Central Government's initiatives to prevent Human Rights Violations.

State Govt. initiative to prevent Human Rights violations.	Central Govt. initiative to prevent Human Rights violations.		Total
	Taking initiative	No initiative	
Taking initiative	74	96	170
	43.5%	56.5%	100.0%
No initiative	27	193	220
	12.3%	87.7%	100.0%
No response	0	1	1
	.0%	100.0%	100.0%
Total	101	290	391
	25.8%	74.2%	100.0%

The above table clearly indicates that 25.8% responded that the Central Govt. is taking the initiative to prevent Human Rights violations and 74.2% responded that the Central Govt. is not taking any initiative to prevent Human Rights violations. On the other hand, 170 responded that State Govt. is taking the initiative to prevent Human Rights violations and 220 responded that State Govt. is not taking any initiatives to prevent Human Rights violations.

In comparing the State Govt. and the Central Govt. initiatives to prevent Human Rights violations, it is found that very little initiative is being taken by the State and Central Govt. to prevent Human Rights violations.

Table no. 10

Information about the most common type of Human Rights Violation.

Most common type of Violation	No. of Respondents	Percent
Body check	73	18.7
House raid	32	8.2
Curfew and bandh	123	31.5
Dragging the suspect	60	15.3
Kidnap	45	11.5
Open firing at public places	55	14.1
Others	3	0.8
Total	391	100.0

The above table clearly indicates that out of 391 respondents, 31.5% responded that the most common type of Violation is the imposition of curfew and bandh. Another 18.7% responded to the random Body check and 15.3% responded to the dragging of the suspects in public places. The rest 0.8% responded to other types of violation.

Hence, it can be concluded that the most common type of violation in the area is the imposition of curfew and bandh, followed by the random body check, dragging of suspects in public places, and open firing at public places.

Table no. 11

Information about the notification and warrant issued before the violence.

Notification and warrant before the violence	No. of Respondents	Percent
Prior notification	51	13.0
No notification	340	87.0
Total	391	100.0

The table clearly indicates that out of 391 respondents, 13.0% responded that prior notification and warrant were issued before the violence but the rest 87.0% responded that there was no notification and no warrant was issued before the violence.

Therefore, this shows that most of the violence was not preceded by any prior notification or warrant.

Table no. 12

Information about the most sufferers of Human Rights Violation.

Most sufferers of Human Rights Violation	No. of Respondents	Percent
Women	81	20.7
Youth	149	38.1
Elders	66	16.9
Village Council	92	23.5
Others	3	0.8
Total	391	100.0

The above table clearly indicates that out of 391 respondents, the most sufferers of human rights violations are the youths, which constitute 38.1%, followed by the Village Council at 23.5% and women at 20.7%. The rest 0.8% did not give any opinion on the suffering resulting from human rights violations.

Therefore, it is concluded that the youths are the most affected by human rights violations, followed by the Village Council and Women.

Figure no. 13

Information about violence as the only means to achieve the goal of the Military.

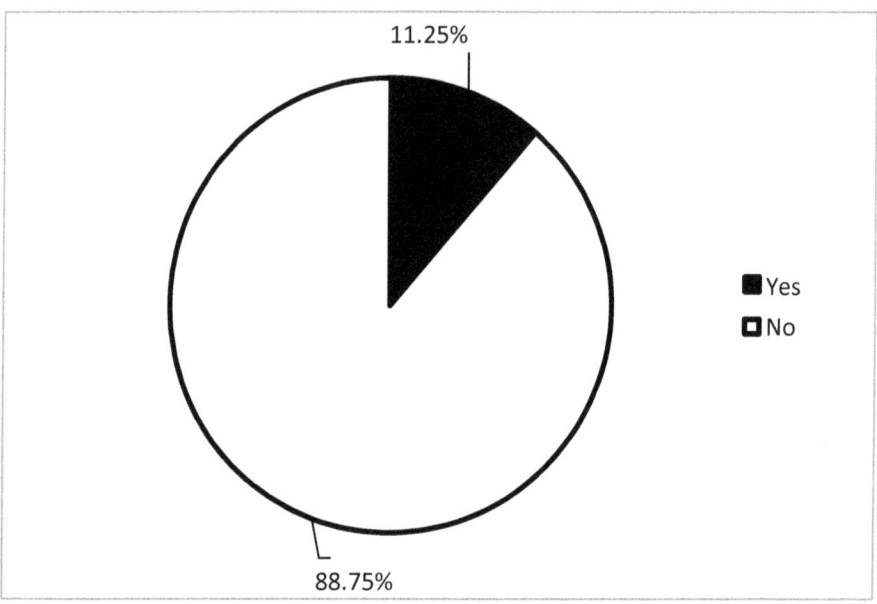

The above Pie chart clearly indicates that out of 391 respondents, 88.75% responded that they did not consider violence as the only means to achieve the goals of the military. Only 11.25% responded that they considered violence as the only means to achieve the goals of the military.

This shows that the majority of the respondents did not consider violence as the only means to achieve the goals of the military. This indicates that the respondents believe in non-violent methods such as diplomacy and negotiations as the primary means to achieve the military's goals.

Table no. 14

Information about the reason for checking vehicles and houses by the Military.

Reason for checking Vehicles and Houses by the Military	No. of Respondents	Percent
Looking for insurgents	110	28.1
Looking for weapons	42	10.7
Looking for suspects	158	40.4
Looking for Drugs and Intoxicants	75	19.2
Others	6	1.5
Total	391	100.0

The above table clearly indicates that out of 391 respondents, 40.4% responded that the reason for checking vehicles and houses by the military is to look out for suspects. The other 28.1% stated that is to look out for insurgents. Only 1.5% did not give other opinions about the reason behind checking vehicles and houses by the military.

Overall, it can be said that the majority of respondents think that the main reason for the military to check vehicles and houses is to look out for suspects and insurgents.

Table no. 15

Opinion about the objective of implementing AFSPA.

Objective of implementing AFSPA	No. of Respondents	Percent
For safety and security	85	21.7
Not for safety and security	303	77.5
No response	3	0.8
Total	391	100.0

The table clearly indicates that out of 391 respondents, only 21.7% responded that the objective of implementing AFSPA is for the safety and security of the civilians but the majority, which consists of 77.5% responded that the objective of implementing AFSPA is not for the safety and security of the civilians. Only 0.8% did not give any opinion about the objective of implementing AFSPA.

Overall, the majority of the respondents do not agree that the objective of implementing AFSPA is for the safety and security of civilians.

Figure no. 16

Information about an increase in violence with the imposition of AFSPA.

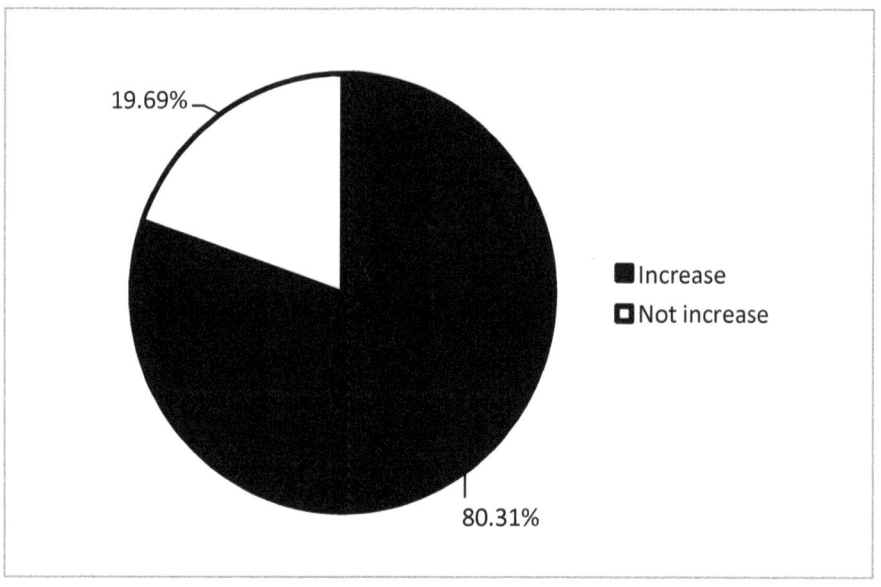

The above Pie chart clearly indicates that out of 391 respondents, 80.31% responded that there is an increase in violence due to the imposition of AFSPA whereas 19.69% responded that there is no increase in violence due to the imposition of AFSPA.

Therefore, this shows that the majority of the respondents believe that the imposition of AFSPA has led to an increase in violence.

Figure no. 17

Information about the response to the violations committed by the Indian Military.

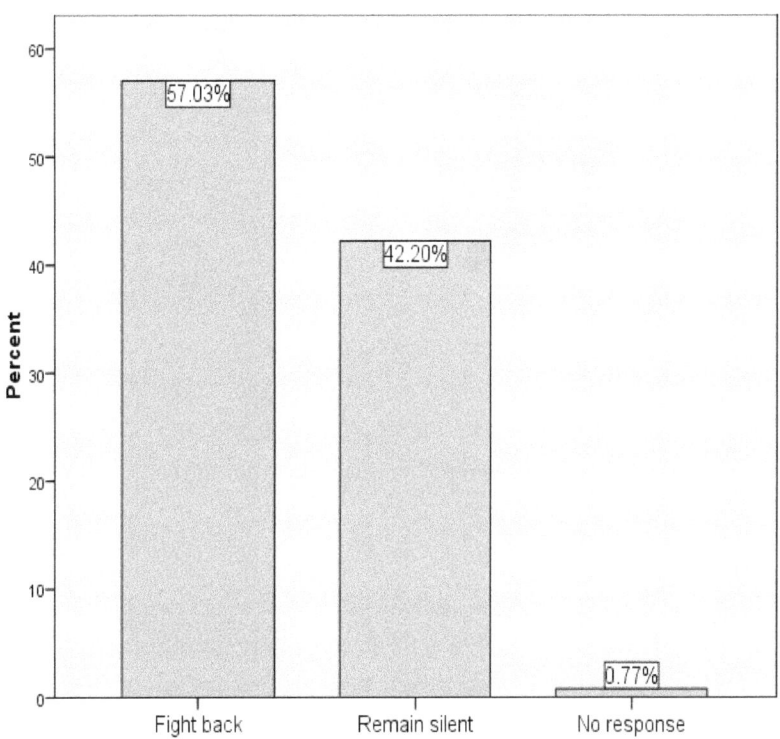

The above Bar chart clearly indicates that out of 391 respondents, 57.03% of the respondents responded that they fight back against the violence committed by the Indian military. The rest 42.20% of the respondents responded that they remained silent. Only 0.77% did not give any opinion on the violence committed by the Indian military.

This clearly shows that people are not happy with the violence committed by the Indian military and are ready to fight back against it. This is an indication of the public opinion and people's desire for justice.

Figure no. 18

Information about the desire to appeal to the government to remove the AFSPA.

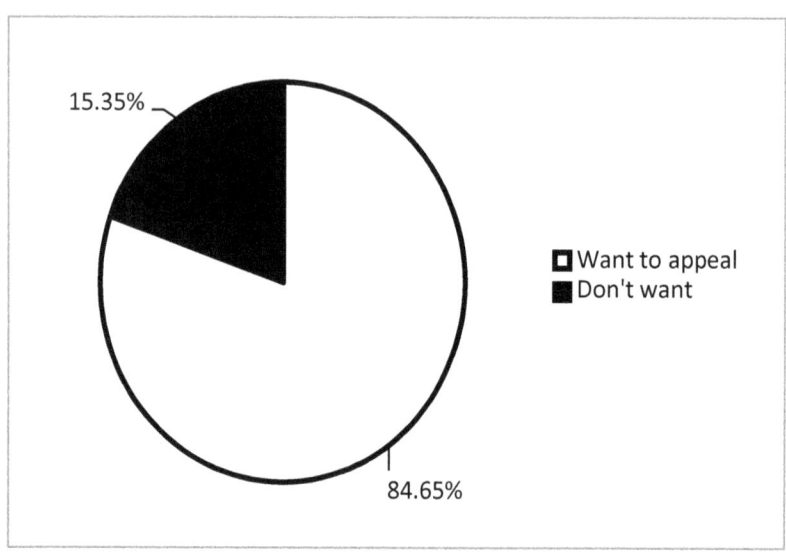

The above Pie chart clearly indicates that out of 391 respondents, most of the respondents, i.e., 84.65% want to appeal to the government to remove the AFSPA but 15.35% don't want to appeal to the government to remove the AFSPA.

Therefore, it is seen that the majority want to appeal to the government to remove the AFSPA.

Table no. 19

Information about the Military abiding by the rules and regulations laid down under AFSPA.

Military abiding by the Rules and Regulations of AFSPA	No. of Respondents	Percent
Abide by the Rules	108	27.6
Not abiding by the Rules	283	72.4
Total	391	100.0

The table clearly indicates that out of 391 respondents, 72.4% responded that the military did not abide by the rules and regulations laid down under AFSPA, and only 27.6% responded that they do abide by the rules and regulations laid down under AFSPA.

Therefore, the majority of respondents were dissatisfied with the military's compliance with AFSPA. This suggests that there is a need for the military to improve its adherence to the rules and regulations laid down under AFSPA.

Table no. 20

Information about the Armed Forces violating the right to life.

Opinion about the violation of the right to life	No. of Respondents	Percent
Agree	175	44.7
Strongly agree	124	31.7
Disagree	55	14.1
Strongly disagree	37	9.5
Total	391	100.0

The above table clearly indicates that out of 391 respondents, most respondents, about 44.7% responded that they agree that the right to life has been violated by the military. And 14.1% responded that they disagree that the right to life has been violated by the military.

Therefore, we can conclude that the majority of the respondents agree that the right to life has been violated by the military.

Table no. 21
Opinion on terrorism is violating Human Rights.

Terrorism is violating Human Rights	No. of Respondents	Percent
Agree	211	53.5
Strongly agree	145	36.8
Disagree	16	3.8
Strongly disagree	19	4.6
No response	5	1.3
Total	391	100.0

The above table clearly indicates that out of 391 respondents, 53.5% of the respondents agree that terrorism is violating human rights, and 3.8% of the respondents disagree that terrorism is violating human rights. Only 1.3% of the respondents did not give any opinion regarding terrorism violating human rights.

Overall, this indicates that a majority of the respondents agree that terrorism is violating human rights.

Figure no. 22

Information about the sparing of women from terrorism.

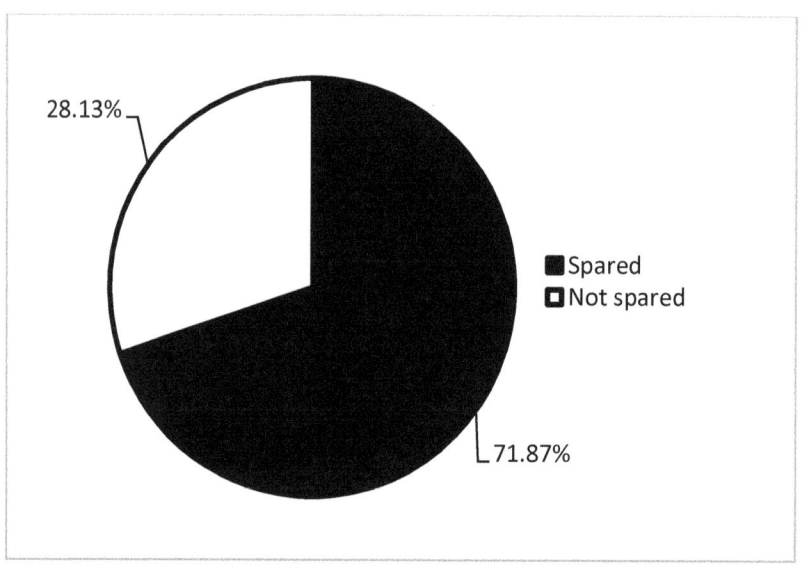

The above Pie chart clearly indicates that out of 391 respondents, 71.87% responded that women were spared from terrorism but 28.13% responded that women were not spared from terrorism.

This shows that women are still not spared from terrorism, even though the majority of respondents believe that they are. This suggests that there is still a need for further efforts to protect women and girls from the effects of terrorism.

Table no. 23

Information about the types of measures taken to stop terrorism.

Type of measures to stop terrorism	No. of Respondents	Percent
Peace rally	280	71.6
Inform to D.C/D.M	30	7.7
Contact the Human Rights Organizations	81	20.7
Total	391	100.0

The above table clearly indicates that out of 391 respondents, 71.6% responded that they organized peace rallies to stop terrorism and 20.7% of respondents contacted human rights organizations to stop terrorism.

Therefore, most of the respondents organized peace rallies, followed by contacting human rights organizations to stop terrorism.

Table no. 24

Information about the impact of violation of human rights.

Impact of violation of human rights	No. of Respondents	Percent
Education	55	14.1
Economy	51	13.0

Religion	48	12.3
Society	233	59.6
No response	4	1.0
Total	391	100.0

The table clearly indicates that out of 391 respondents, 59.6% responded that the violation of human rights has affected society, and 14.1% responded that the violation of human rights has affected education. Only 1.0% did not give any opinion on the impact of violation of human rights. Violation of human rights has impacted all aspects of life; economy, education, religion, and society.

Therefore, the violation of human rights has negatively impacted on Tangkhul community.

Table no. 25

Information about the response given by police to the complaints about terrorism.

Response of Police to complaints about terrorism	No. of Respondents	Percent
Positive response	149	38.1
Negative response	242	61.9
Total	391	100.0

The above table clearly indicates that out of 391 respondents, 61.9% responded that the police gave a negative response when people filed complaints about terrorism, and 38.1% responded that the police gave a positive response when people filed complaints about terrorism.

This suggests that the police are not taking people's complaints about terrorism seriously and are not responding to them in a timely or effective manner.

Figure no. 26

Information about the acceptance of the military for their mistakes and destruction committed.

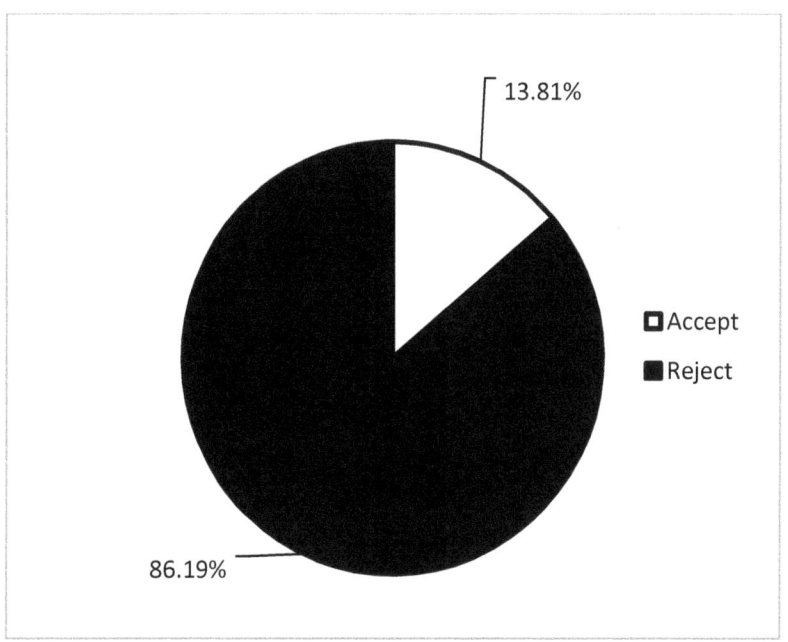

The above Pie chart clearly indicates that out of 391 respondents, 86.19% responded that the military rejects the mistakes and destruction committed by them, and 13.81% responded that the military accepts the mistakes and destruction committed by them.

Therefore, it can be concluded that the majority of respondents believe that the military rejects the mistakes and destruction committed by them.

Figure no. 27

Information about terrorism being a threat to Tangkhul traditional culture.

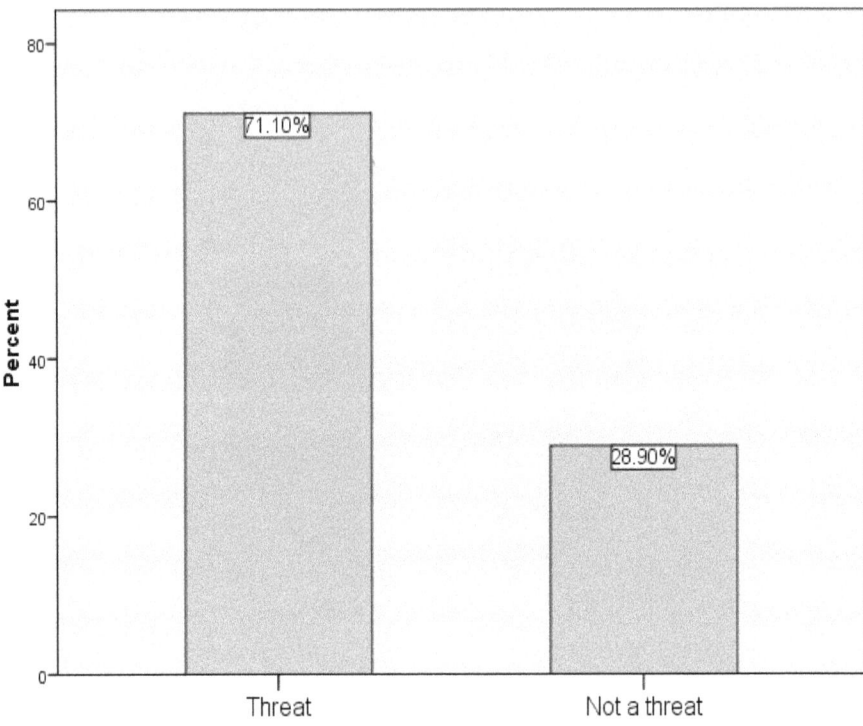

The above Bar chart clearly indicates that out of 391 respondents, 71.10% responded that terrorism is a threat to the Tangkhul traditional culture and 28.90% responded that terrorism is not a threat to the Tangkhul traditional culture.

Therefore, it can be concluded that the majority of respondents believe that terrorism is a threat to the Tangkhul traditional culture.

Table no. 28

Information about the effects of violating human rights.

Effect of violating human rights	No. of Respondents	Percent
Emotional effect	41	10.5
Mental effect	138	35.3
Physical effect	210	53.7
Others	2	0.5
Total	391	100.0

The above table clearly indicates that out of 391 respondents, 53.7% responded that they were affected physically due to violation of human rights, 35.3% responded that they were affected mentally due to violation of human rights, 10.5 % responded that they were affected emotionally, and 0.5 % responded to other types of effects caused due to violating human rights.

It can be concluded that physical and mental effects were the most common effects among the respondents due to violation of human rights, while emotional and other types of effects were less common.

Table no. 29

Information about the effects of physical punishment.

Effect of physical punishment	No. of Respondents	Percent
Fracture of bones	13	3.3
Physical pain	54	13.8
Handicap	71	18.2
Health weakening	117	29.9
Reduced lifespan	135	34.5
Others	1	0.3
Total	391	100.0

The table clearly indicates that out of 391 respondents, 34.5% responded that their lifespan was shortened due to physical punishment given by the Armed Forces. 29.9% responded that their health weakened and some 0.3 % responded other types of harm are brought due to physical punishment given by the Armed Forces.

It can be concluded that physical punishment given by the Armed Forces has a significant impact on the health and lifespan of the respondents.

Table no. 30

Information about the Armed Forces' understanding of the sentiments of the civilians.

Armed Forces' understanding of the sentiments of the civilians	No. of Respondents	Percent
Understand	74	18.9
Don't understand	317	81.1
Total	391	100.0

The above table clearly indicates that out of 391 respondents, only 18.9 % responded that the Armed Forces understand the sentiments of the respondents and 81.1 % responded that the Armed Forces do not understand the sentiments of the civilians.

Therefore, it can be concluded that mostly the Armed Forces do not understand the sentiments of the civilians.

Figure no. 31

Information about Armed Forces providing compensation for damage.

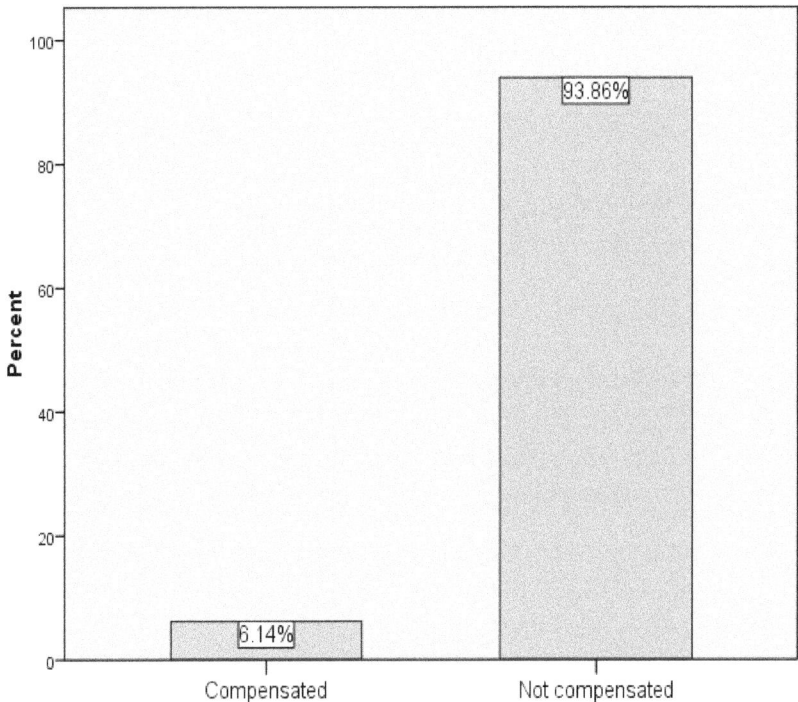

The above Bar chart clearly indicates that out of 391 respondents, only 6.14 % responded that the Armed Forces provided compensation for the damage done by them and 93.86 % responded that the Armed Forces did not provide compensation.

Therefore, it can be concluded that mostly the Armed Forces did not provide compensation for the damage done by them.

Table no. 32

Information about the reaction when the Armed Forces conducted a body search and luggage check.

Reaction when the Armed Forces did a body search and luggage check	No. of Respondents	Percent
Does not bother	32	8.2
Not comfortable	359	91.8
Total	391	100.0

The above table clearly indicates that out of 391 respondents, only 8.2 % responded that they did not bother when the Armed Forces conducted body search and luggage check and 91.8 % did not feel comfortable when the Armed Forces conducted body search and luggage check.

This shows that people generally do not feel comfortable when their bodies and luggage are checked by the Armed Forces.

Figure no. 33

Information about the effect of human rights violation on the religious ethics of Christianity.

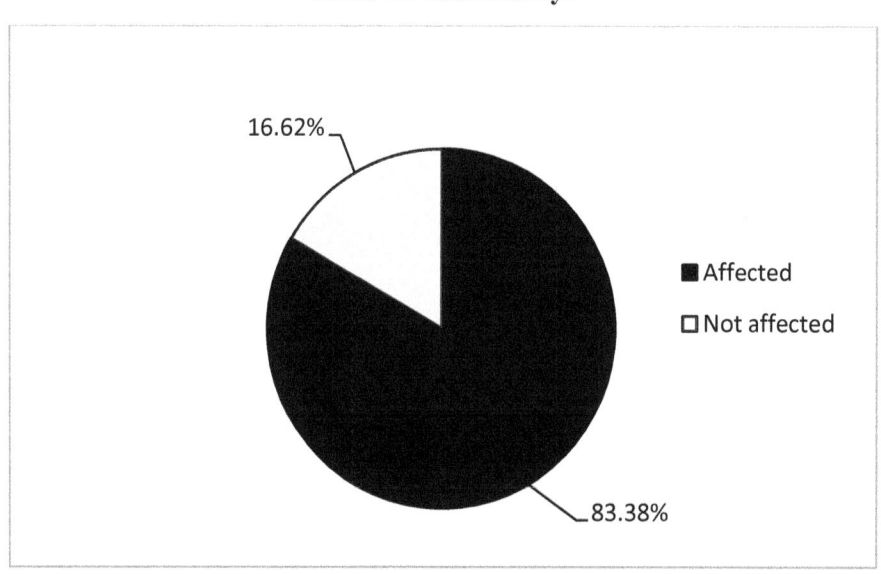

The above Pie chart clearly indicates that out of 391 respondents, 83.38 % responded that human rights violations have affected the religious ethics of Christianity and 16.62 % responded that violation did not affect the religious ethics of Christianity.

Therefore, it can be concluded that human rights violation has a major impact on the religious ethics of Christianity.

Table no. 34

Information about the main cause of Terrorism in Ukhrul District.

Main cause of Terrorism in Ukhrul District	No. of Respondents	Percent
Due to AFSPA	61	15.6
Misuse of power	265	67.8
Suppressing the Insurgency	62	15.9
Other reason	3	.8
Total	391	100.0

The above table clearly indicates that out of 391 respondents, 67.8 % responded that the main cause of terrorism is due to misuse of power,

15.9 % responded that it is due to suppression of insurgency, 15.6 % responded that it is due to AFSPA, and only 0.8 % responded that it is due to other reasons in Ukhrul district.

Therefore, it can be concluded that the main cause of terrorism in Ukhrul district is the misuse of power.

Table no. 35

Opinion on Terrorism brought psychological effects on the community.

Terrorism brought psychological effects on the community	No. of Respondents	Percent
Effect	379	96.9
No effect	12	3.1
No response	1	.3
Total	391	100.0

The table clearly indicates that out of 391 respondents, 96.9 % responded that terrorism has brought negative effects on the psychology of the community, 3.1 % responded that terrorism did not bring negative psychological effects on the community, and 0.3 % respondents did not give any opinion in this regard.

Thus, the majority of the respondents believe that terrorism has brought negative psychological effects on the community.

Table no. 36

Information about Civil Organizations taking initiative to stop terrorism.

Civil Organizations initiative to stop terrorism	No. of Respondents	Percent
Taking initiative	332	84.9
No initiative	58	14.8
No response	1	.3
Total	391	100.0

The above table clearly shows that out of 391 respondents, 84.9% responded that Civil organizations are taking initiatives to stop terrorism, 14.8% responded that Civil organizations are not taking any initiative to stop terrorism, and 0.3% respondents did not respond.

Overall, it can be concluded that most of the respondents believe that Civil organizations are taking initiatives to stop terrorism.

Table no. 37

Information about measures to reduce terrorism.

Measures to reduce terrorism	No. of Respondents	Percent
Removal of AFSPA	69	17.6
Respecting Human Rights	254	65.0
Stop misusing power	60	15.3
Evacuation of Military	7	1.8
Others	1	.3
Total	391	100.0

The above table clearly shows that out of 391 respondents, 17.6% responded that the means to reduce terrorism is removal of AFSPA, 65.0% responded that respecting Human rights will reduce terrorism, and 1.8% responded that evacuation of the military. Only 0.3% responded to other opinions about reducing terrorism.

Overall, the majority of the respondents believe that respecting Human rights will reduce terrorism.

Figure no. 38

Information about the participation of womenfolk in stopping terrorism.

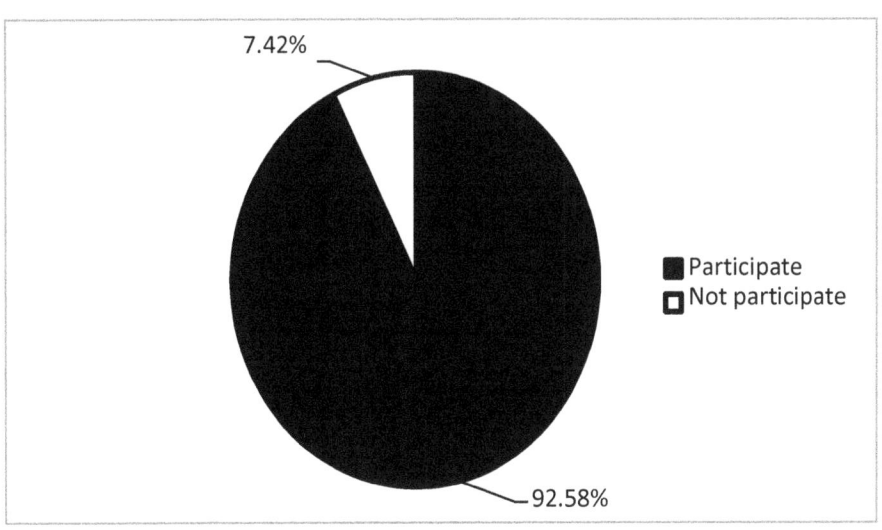

The above Pie chart clearly shows that out of 391 respondents, 92.58% responded that womenfolk participated in stopping terrorism and 7.42% responded that womenfolk did not participate in stopping terrorism.

Therefore, it can be concluded that the majority of the womenfolk do participate in stopping terrorism.

Figure no. 39

Information about the intervention of police in preventing violence.

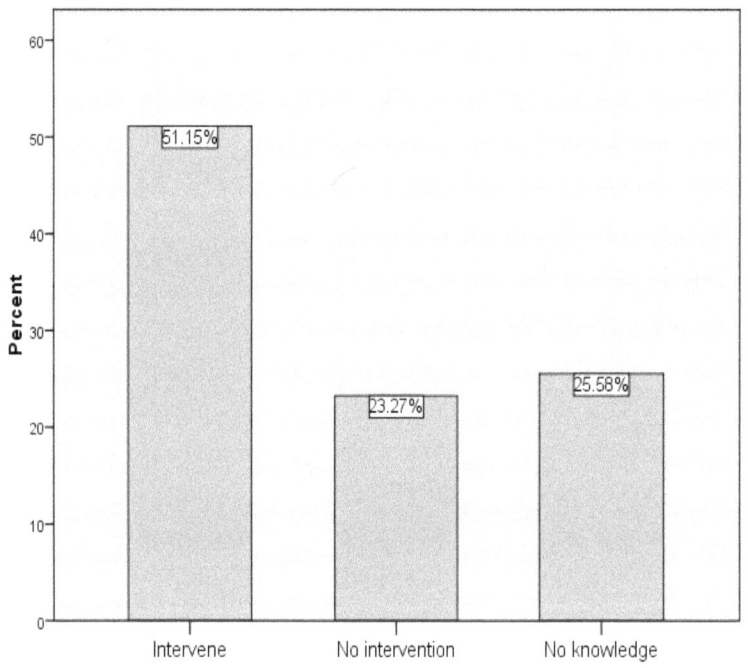

The above Bar chart clearly shows that out of 391 respondents, 51.15% responded that police intervened to prevent violence and 23.27% responded that police did not intervene to prevent violence. 25.58% of respondents did not have any knowledge about the intervention of the police to prevent violence.

It can be inferred that the majority of respondents reported that the police did intervene to prevent violence.

Table no. 40

Information about the relationship between Human Rights Activists and the Military.

Relationship between Human Rights activists and the Military	No. of Respondents	Percent
Good relationship	115	29.4
No relationship	273	69.8
No response	3	0.8
Total	391	100.0

The above table clearly shows that out of 391 respondents, 29.4% responded that Human Rights Activists and the Armed Forces have a good relationship, and 69.8% responded that Human Rights Activists and the Armed Forces did not have a good relationship. Only 0.8% of respondents did not have any knowledge about the relationship between Human Rights Activists and the Armed Forces.

Overall, most respondents were of the opinion that the relationship between Human Rights Activists and the Armed Forces was not positive

Figure no. 41
Information about the Indian Military respecting Human Rights laws.

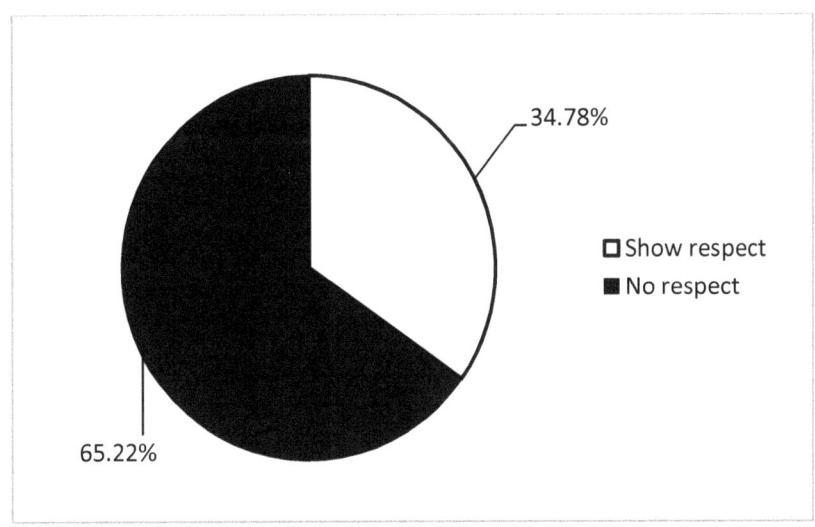

The above Pie chart clearly shows that out of 391 respondents, 34.78% responded that the Indian military showed respect for Human rights laws and 65.22% responded that the Indian military did not respect Human rights laws.

This shows that the majority of the respondents do not believe that the Indian military respects Human rights laws.

Table no. 42

Information about being threatened by the Military when initiating Human Rights Movement.

Threatened by Military when initiating Human Rights Movement	No. of Respondents	Percent
Threatened	308	78.75
Not threatened	83	21.25
Total	391	100.0

The above table clearly shows that out of 391 respondents, 78.75% responded that the Indian military threatened them when initiating Human rights movement and 21.25% responded that the Indian military did not threaten them when initiating Human rights movement.

This shows that the Indian military has a tendency to threaten individuals and organizations when trying to initiate Human rights movement.

Table no.43

Information about the participation of Women in the Human Rights Movement.

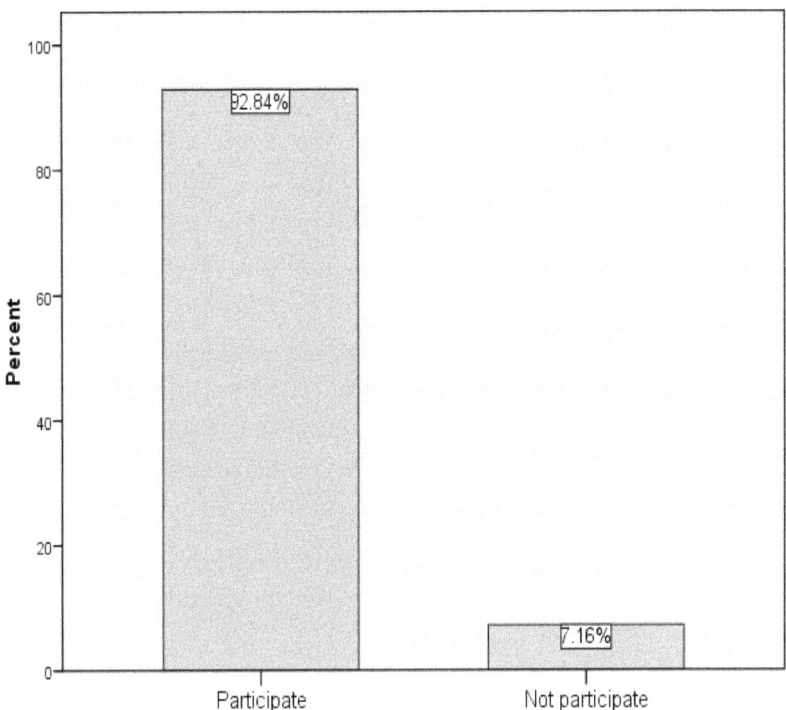

The above Bar chart clearly shows that out of 391 respondents, 98.84% responded that women participated in the Human rights movement and 7.16% responded that women did not participate in the Human rights movement.

This indicates that most people agree with the idea that women are an important part of the Human rights movement.

Table no. 44

Information about the effectiveness of the Human Rights Commission in Ukhrul District.

Effectiveness of Human Rights Commission in Ukhrul District	No. of Respondents	Percent
Effective	89	22.8
Not effective	100	25.6
Don't know	196	50.1
No response	6	1.5
Total	391	100.0

The above table clearly shows that out of 391 respondents, 22.8% responded that Human Rights Commission in Ukhrul District is effective, 25.6% responded that Human Rights Commission in Ukhrul District is not effective, and 50.1% responded that they did not know anything about Human Rights Commission in Ukhrul District while 1.5 % respondents did not respond.

Hence, it can be concluded that the majority of the respondents were unaware of the role played by the Human Rights Commission in Ukhrul District.

Figure no. 45
Opinion that Human Rights Movement can stop terrorism.

The above Pie chart clearly shows that out of 391 respondents, 82.61%

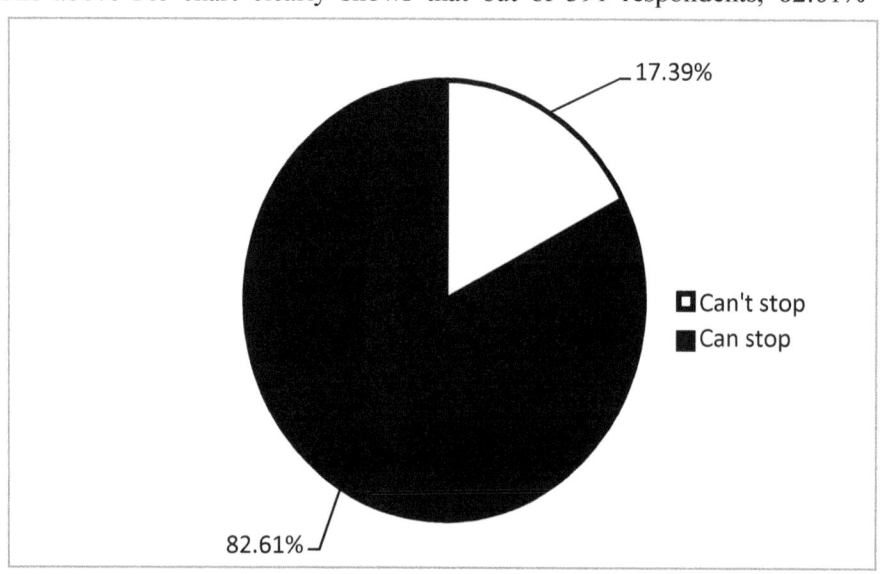

responded that Human rights movement can stop terrorism and 17.39% responded that Human rights movement cannot stop terrorism.

Thus, the majority of the respondents believe that the Human rights movement has the potential to stop terrorism.

Table no. 46

Information about reporting to Social Activists for assistance.

Reporting to Social Activists for assistance	No. of Respondents	Percent
Reported	178	45.5
Not reported	213	54.5
Total	391	100.0

The table clearly shows that out of 391 respondents, 45.5% responded that they reported to Social Activists for assistance and 54.5% responded that they did not report to any Social Activist for assistance.

Therefore, the majority of the respondents did not report to any Social Activist for assistance.

Table no. 47

Information about the response given by Social Activists for assistance.

Response from social activists	No. of Respondents	Percent
Positive response	248	63.4
Negative response	143	36.6
Total	391	100.0

The above table clearly shows that out of 391 respondents, 63.4% responded that social activists give a positive response when approached for assistance and 36.6% responded that social activists do not give a positive response when approached for assistance.

Overall, it can be seen that most social activists do give a positive response when approached for assistance but there is still a significant minority that does not.

Table no. 48

Information about Social workers intervening in social crisis.

Social workers intervening in social crisis	No. of Respondents	Percent
Wants intervention	354	90.5
Don't want	37	9.5
Total	391	100.0

The table clearly shows that out of 391 respondents, 90.5% responded that they want the intervention of social workers in social crisis and 9.5% responded that they did not want the intervention of social workers in social crisis.

Overall, most respondents agreed that social workers should be involved in social crises. This indicates that there is a need for social workers in such situations, as their expertise can be highly beneficial in resolving complex social issues.

Table no. 49

Information about the need for training to equip themselves and defend from human rights violations.

Need for training to equip themselves and defend from human rights violation	No. of Respondents	Percent
Needed	374	95.7
Not needed	17	4.3
Total	391	100.0

The above table clearly shows that out of 391 respondents, 95.7% responded that there is a need for training individuals to defend themselves from human rights violations and 4.3% responded that they do not need training to defend themselves from human rights violations.

This result indicates that most people understand the importance of training to defend themselves from human rights violations and are willing to take steps to protect their rights.

Table no. 50

Information about the views in collaboration with NGOs for solving human rights violation problems.

Collaboration with NGOs to solve human rights violation problems	No. of Respondents	Percent
Want to collaborate	365	93.4
No need	24	6.1
No response	2	.5
Total	391	100.0

The above table clearly shows that out of 391 respondents, 93.4% responded that they wanted to collaborate with NGOs for solving human rights violation problems and 6.1% responded that they did not want to collaborate with NGOs for solving human rights violation problems while 0.5% did not respond.

Therefore, it can be concluded that most of the respondents wanted to collaborate with NGOs to solve human rights violation problems.

Table no. 51

Information about expectations from social workers.

Expectation from social worker	No. of Respondents	Percent
Initiating peace	124	31.7
Giving training	49	12.5
Releasing social tension	26	6.6
Bringing social change	192	49.1
Total	391	100.0

The table clearly shows that out of 391 respondents, 49.1% responded that they expect social workers to bring social change, and 31.7% responded that they expect social workers to initiate a peace process. Only 6.6% of respondents expect social workers to release social tension.

It is evident that the majority of respondents believe that social workers should bring social change, while the least number of respondents believe that social workers should release social tension.

Figure no. 52

Information about the opinion of the Military towards social workers' intervention plea for justice.

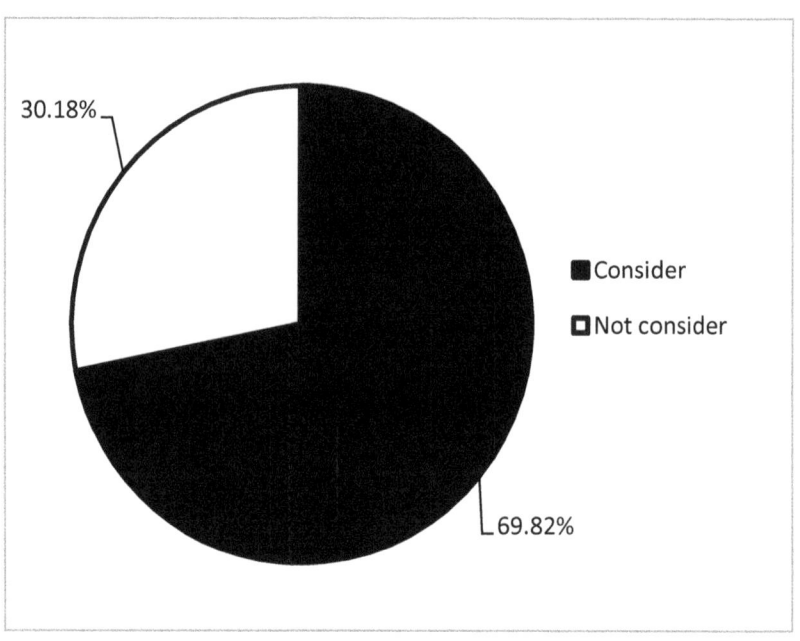

The above Pie chart clearly shows that out of 391 respondents, 69.82% responded that the Indian Military would consider social workers' intervention plea for justice and 30.18% responded that the Indian Military would not consider social workers' intervention plea for justice.

Therefore, we can conclude that the majority of respondents believe that the Indian Military will consider social workers' intervention plea for justice.

Figure no. 53

Information about opinions for NGOs to conduct seminars for women empowerment.

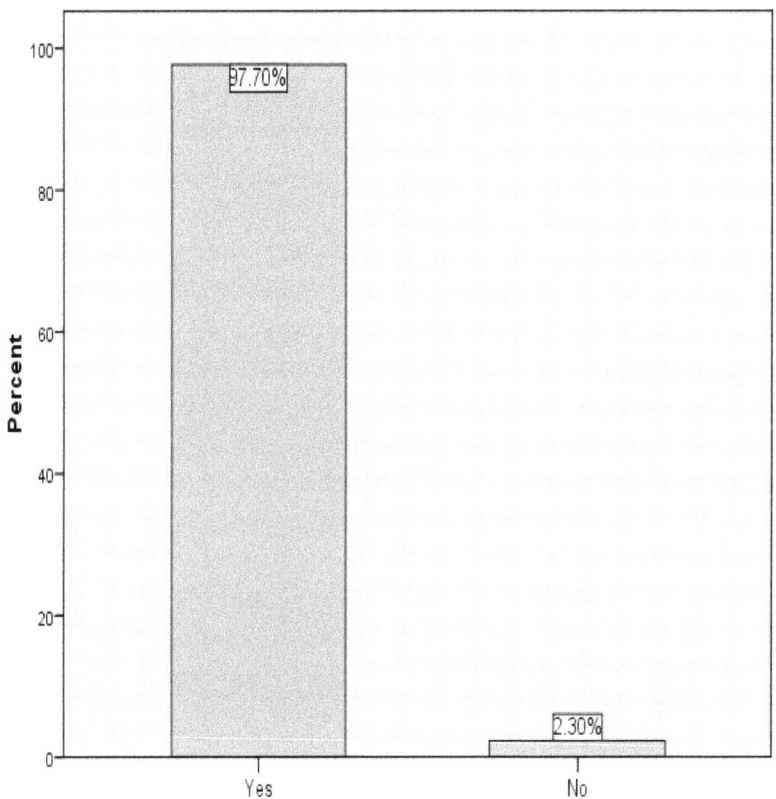

NGO to conduct seminar for women empowerment

The above Bar chart clearly shows that out of 391 respondents, 97.70 % responded that they want NGOs to conduct seminars for women empowerment, and only 2.30 % did not want NGOs to conduct seminars for women empowerment.

Hence, it is clear that the majority of the respondents support the idea of NGOs conducting seminars for women's empowerment.

16

STATE GOVERNMENT ACTION AGAINST HUMAN RIGHTS VIOLATION

The population of Manipur is 2.6 million and there are around 100,000 Indian Armed Forces posted in the state, excluding Manipur state police commando. It seems Manipur state government is just an extension of the central government. For more than 50 years, AFSPA is effectively implemented and the state government seems to be a mere watchdog without democratic participation in several issues. The state government itself has been difficult to understand and cope with the AFSPA, raising questions about why a militarized form of governance is necessary when the state is already capable of handling the situation. However, the state government does not deny the advice and suggestions given by the Central government to look after the problems of human rights violations.

Manipur Government has been trying to bring solutions and minimize the violations happening over the decades. Despite imposing AFSP Act, Manipur has more than 50 armed groups operating in the state and it has always been a "conflict zone" since the 1970s. It is difficult for the Manipur government to deal with all the demands of these armed groups but the State government has been trying its best to maintain peace with all the armed groups. Despite this initiative made by the State government, several human rights violators have provoked economic blockage, bandh, and attacked civilians as well as government offices. Those agitators and human rights violators are detained and given necessary action as per the law by the Manipur government. Meanwhile, several measures were taken to solve the problem of human rights violations that affect the livelihood of the community.

Manipur human rights defenders have a strong concern for the continuous human rights violations and enforcement of the Armed Forces (Special Powers) Act, which has resulted in gross human rights violations in the state for decades. Meanwhile, the report forwarded by the Manipur government to the apex court has prompted human rights activists to the fresh demands for special investigation and justice for nearly 1700 extrajudicial killings over the past 35 years. Immediate withdrawal of the AFSPA from the Northeast state is also strongly demanded. A well- known human rights activist, Irom Chanu Sharmila, the 'Iron Lady of Manipur' who fought for the removal of the Armed Forces Special Powers Act, 1958 from Manipur state through a hunger strike for 16 long years long was overlooked.

The Oinam village (Senapati district) incident of 9th July 1987 can never be erased from the mind of every sensible citizen of the state. Every child of Oinam has a story to tell when recounting the nightmarish story of 'Operation Blue Bird 1987'. On that fateful day suspected NSCN (National Socialist Council of Nagaland) raided the Assam Rifles outpost at Oinam killing nine soldiers were killed in the attack and injuring three others. It is allegedly reported that NSCN stole 128 SLR, 18 LMG, 4 two-inch Mortar, 400 Grenades, 20 Carbine Sten, 1,28,000 rounds of ammunition, and two wireless sets. In retaliation to this, the Assam Rifles launched Operation Bluebird for four months of inhuman torture, house raids, grouping of villages, slave labor, sexual harassment, and assault on women. The NPMHR in their petition filed in October 1987 to the Guwahati High Court, alleged that the security forces committed the following cognizable offenses: infliction of grievous injuries, manslaughter, murder, rape and sexual harassment, looting and theft, desecration of the church, arson, wanton destruction of private, public properties; including school buildings, illegal raids, illegal evictions, seizures, forced labour, illegal detentions, and arrests.

Around thirty villages experienced the unjust bitterness of the Armed Forces, 112 houses were dismantled, 125 residents' houses are allegedly burnt, 6 schools and 10 churches were dismantled, seven villages' properties worth Rs.50,75,000/- were looted, 5 villages were forced to work, 27 persons are alleged to have been killed in the encounter on different dates in Senapati District, 5 women were sexually molested 3 women were raped and 300 persons are alleged to have been tortured by Armed Forces (Assam Rifles) as recapitulated by the Naga People's Movement for Human Rights.

The report stated in the booklet, 'Post Torture State of Mental Health' written by seven doctors from outside Manipur got to write, 'Torture is a cruel, inhuman degradation of one human being by another.' Among the

104 victims studied by them, the high prevalence of Post Traumatic Stress Disorders (PTSD) correlates with the torture inflicted in the incident. From the study, it is found that 38.61% of the victims still suffer from recurrent dreams of torture and 66.33% have disturbed sleep. 54.44% are incapable of enjoying village festivals, friendships, food, and sex life. 37.62% have lost their self-confidence and developed a sense of an insecure future.

The Oinam villagers spread across the country commemorate every 9th of July as a day of 'Onae Reh Dah - Great Battle of Oinam' in prayers. As a result of launching Operation Bluebird 1987, the village is never the same as before mar with the killing of great leaders, gross human rights violations, atrocities, damaged and looted properties, torturing men and women nefariously turning the surroundings and whole village to a land of nightmare and horror. The unforgettable incident and the misuse of power and unconstitutional amendment by the Armed Forces is still unforgivable to this day by the people of Oinam.

To look after the human rights violations, several attempts have been made and a commission of inquiry has been set up to look into the violence committed because of the Armed Forces Special Powers Act in Manipur. The Commission was formed with the idea of Ashoka Fellows Collin Gonsalves and Babloo Loitongbam to conduct an Independent people's inquiry through his organization Human Rights Alert (HRA) and other human rights activists at Imphal. They invited Justice H. Suresh, former Judge of the Bombay High Court to lead the Commission. To constitute the details of the work of the commission, a Preparatory Committee was formed. Mr. A.C. Sharma was appointed as the Convener and Mr. Babloo Loitongbam as the Co-convener. The Commission met with the victims of human rights violations like rape, torment, and the families of the ones who were forced to disappear and those who were randomly killed, and examined the previous reports of the official commissions of investigation and the cases taken up by the "Manipur Human Rights Commission." Meetings and several dialogues were conducted with civil organizations, human rights activists, well-known lawyers, and other responsible individuals in the state.

Manipur State Human Rights Commission, which was established in 1998, under the Protection of Human Rights Act, 1993 along with the appointment of a Chairperson and Members for the first term. Manipur Human Rights Commission (MHRC) has been monitoring all the human rights violation cases, investigating the cases, and protecting human rights from time to time. The second term was functional from May 2005 to May 2010.[37] The Commission was doing well but it did not last long as the "Manipur State Human Rights Commission" became defunct in May 2010 due to a lack of quorum. Several Human rights activists and civil organizations say there was a glimmer of hope among the people of Manipur when the state government incepted MHRC in 1998. Despite its failure, the then Chief Minister Okram Ibobi Singh assured to revive the Manipur Human Rights Commission but couldn't do much. It is the concern of the State government to revive the Manipur State Human Rights Commission to preserve harmony and peace in the state. Due to the dysfunction of MHRC human rights violation cases are mounting in owe.

A section of the Manipuris feels that the power to declare an area disturbed should remain solely with the state government, not with the Governor. The 1972 version of AFSPA extended the same power to declare an area disturbed concurrently to the central government. In recent years, with the initiatives of the present Chief Minister, N. Biren Singh, Manipur Human Rights Commission is reviving and AFSPA has been revoked from some valley districts. A glimmer of hope is emerging and it will be of immense help to the poor sections of the society who are commonly victims of human rights violations by the Armed forces. But sadly, to date, regular Chairperson of Manipur Human Rights Commission is yet to be appointed.

---

[37] https://thefrontiermanipur.com/hc-pulls-up-manipur-govt-gives-10-days-to-initiate-process-to-appoint-mhrc-chief/#:~:text=Khaidem%20Mani%20was%20appointed%20the,order%20on%20January%204%2C%202018.

17

CIVIL SOCIETY ORGANIZATIONS' INTERVENTION IN HUMAN RIGHTS VIOLATION

Tangkhul village has been considered a sovereign, republic, and democratic village by itself since time immemorial. The administrative setup and the governance of the Tangkhul community are democratic in nature. The Tangkhul community exercises their own rights within their jurisdiction and anything against humanity is not tolerated. Since the imposition of AFSPA in 1958 by the parliament of India in Manipur, the situation has become very tense and the image of human rights has been damaged by the Armed Forces. Peace and harmony in the community have been shattered after the imposition of the CrPC Act in the district. Individuals have been denied their freedom and rights by the CrPC Act resulting in the piling up of human rights violation cases in the district.

The Tangkhul community has strongly reacted against the imposition of AFSPA and CrPC. Several protests and rallies have been carried out in the district, led by the highest apex bodies Tangkhul Katamnao Saklong (TKS), Tangkhul Mayar Ngala Long (TMNL), Tangkhul Naga Long (TNL) and Tangkhul Shanao Long (TSL). Civil organizations and the community have raised their voices at various state and central levels that are strongly supported by the Naga People's Movement for Human Rights (NPMHR), Naga Student Federation (NSF), All Naga Student Association Manipur (ANSAM), All Manipur Student Union (AMSU), and Naga Hoho. All the local civil organizations, NGOs and Institutions, Religious organizations, and the community at large jointly raised their voice together to the state government for the atrocities committed by the Armed forces in the district. Removal of AFSPA from the state is the sole objective for all the concerned organizations and it has been appealed to the central government multiple times.

Tangkhul community has been living in a dark corner of human rights violation, and due to their ignorance about their rights, they have been deprived of all aspects of human rights. For decades, the Armed forces have committed several crimes against women in the district. The community somehow has come up with the courage to fight for justice, and in some cases, the culprits were reprimanded and punished accordingly. Yet, many cases are not being investigated by the concerned authority.

Despite the state government's negligence, the community civil organization is taking the initiative to investigate and bring them before the court. The Tangkhul community is tired of atrocities meted out to them and is struggling to survive under the shadow of the Armed Forces. With the imposition of the AFSP Act in Ukhrul, civilians have been deprived of their rights and their plea for justice has been falling on deaf ears. Even so, to date, there is no sign of waning in fighting for justice.

Tangkhul Naga Long (TNL) intervention in Conflict Mitigation[38]

Tangkhul Naga Long (TNL) is the guardian of the Tangkhl Naga Community and is one of the biggest federations of the Tangkhul community. It is the highest apex body of the Tangkhul Naga community at the Tribe level. The Tangkhul Naga Long was formed before the Second World War but its constitution was later adopted after the official formation of the Tangkhul Wungnao Long (Tangkhul Kingship Forum). Tangkhul Naga Long is not a Government body, political body, social organization, or NGO. Rather, it is a tribal apex body of the Tangkhul Naga community under the customary system of the Tangkhul Naga community. Most of the social and political organizations began in the village community and it was formed according to the Tangkhul Naga community's traditional institutions, which evolved naturally since ancient times.

The Tangkhul Naga Long was formed by the Tangkhul Naga community with the following objectives:

i. To legislate laws and norms
ii. Preserve the history of the Tangkhul Naga community.
iii. Uphold the solidarity of all the Tangkhul Naga community.

---

[38] https://kharingyoshimrah01.wordpress.com/2016/04/13/the-social-structure-of-tangkhul-naga/

iv. Protect and safeguard the Tangkhul Naga community from war or attacks from outsiders.

iv. Response to emerging situations and issues.

v. Protect and defend Tangkhul territories.

vi. Deal TNL court case and resolve conflict.

vii. Execute /Support Decision of United Naga Council & Naga Hoho

There are four historical longphang (court) in Ukhrul district; any conflicts are settled in their own area longphang according to the geographical location. However, if there is a dispute on the verdicts among the Longphang or if the accused or victim or petitioner is not satisfied with the verdict, then they approach the Longrei (which is the apex court of the Tangkhul Naga community).

The apex body has four Longphang (Court):

i. Ato (North) Longphang

ii. Aze (South) Longphang

iii. Zingtun (West) Longphang

iv. Zingsho (East) Longphang

Tangkhul Shanao Long (TSL) intervention on Human Rights Violation.[39]

Formation of Tangkhul Shanao Long (TSL):

Tangkhul Shanao Long (TSL) was formed in 1974 after several incidents of humiliation, inhuman torment, and ill-treatment by the Indian Armed Forces. The incidents of 3rd March 1974, in which the villages of Kumram and Grihang were intensely operated by the 95 Border Security Force (BSF) led to the foundation of the Tangkhul Shanao Long (TSL).

Miss Rose Ningshen from Kumram is one of the rape victims and this rape incident is one of the many incidents committed by the Indian Armed Forces. The Armed Forces have been behaving like beasts towards Tangkhul women for decades. To respond to such kind of inhuman behavior towards women, the women of Tangkhul realized the need to form a

---

[39] https://www.facebook.com/media/set/?set=a.404432026287751.96106.382340 698496884&type=1&l=9df6eca75c

Women's Union so that they could jointly fight back together and voice their grievances at a higher level. They knew that unless such a group unified, Tangkhul women would continue to face humiliation and discrimination. It was on 4th March 1974 that the "East District Women Association (EDWA)" was formed. Ms. Masophi Luithui was appointed as the first President. Later, East District Women was renamed as 'Tangkhul Shanao Long'. Since then, Tangkhul Shanao Long has been intensely active in the Human rights movement and has protected civilians from the Armed Forces.

The Tangkhul Shanao Long (TSL) is the highest apex body of all women's organizations of Tangkhul community in Ukhrul district. The motive for its formation was to fight against the incidents of humiliation and inhuman treatment of Tangkhul women by the Indian Armed Forces in the district.

Apart from safeguarding women's rights, dignity, and modesty, the Tangkhul Shanao Long (TSL) Shanao Long also took up other important issues affecting the social system; drugs and alcohol were banned in the district and Shanao Long volunteers literally took the task of checking the import of drugs and alcohol in Ukhrul district. Apart from human rights movement and developmental work, Shanao Long also conducted seminars relating to women's issues, organized sports to enhance sportsmanship, and gave awards for excellence in education. They also promote peace, economic upliftment, and improvement of livelihood. They also look into human rights issues, human trafficking, environmental awareness, etc. The Tangkhul women play an important role as Peacemaker/Mediator known as "Phakhreila or Pukreila".

All the women's society of the Tangkhul community village is a unit of Tangkhul Shanao Long (TSL), it has around twenty thousand total members. The active members of Tangkhul Shanao Long (TSL) are aged fifteen years and above. Out of 260 odd Tangkhul community villages, almost all the villages are affiliated units of Tangkhul Shanao Long (TSL) except for a few villages.

The President of Tangkhul Shanao Long (TSL) is the Chief Functionary and spokesperson of the organization. She is appointed as a full-time worker and is assisted by the General Secretary, who is also a full-time worker, along with the executive committee members. Apart from this, there is a General Body that consists of all registered members. The General Body meets at least twice in a calendar year and the Executive Committee meets at least seven times in a calendar year or more than that as per the situation or as per the needs. The General Body has the final authority to make any decisions and draft any major policy of the Tangkhul Shanao Long (TSL) even though the Executive Committee executes day-to-day activities and programs of the Tangkhul Shanao Long (TSL).

Aims & Objectives of TSL:
i. To safeguard the rights, dignity, and modesty of women
ii. To promote the cultural, customary life of women, and education.
iii. To promote economic growth and welfare of the total livelihood, which includes handicrafts, animal husbandry, agriculture, tailoring, weaving, etc.
iv. To promote peace, growth, development, and prosperity in every respect.
v. To maintain and create a healthy environment in life.
vi. To establish rapport with other organizations with similar objectives all over the globe.
vii. To create awareness among the villagers by organizing and conducting training, seminars, consultations, workshops, etc.
viii. To participate in maintaining ecology and balancing the environment.
ix. To organize relief, charity, and grants for whoever is in genuine need due to natural calamities and unforeseen incidents.

Programme Activities:

Due to the unavailability of good resources and financial backups, Tangkhul Shanao Long has not been able to execute much of what it had planned, but still, various programs and activities have been undertaken such as:

i. Giving relief and assistance to the victims of human rights violations inflicted by the Indian Armed Forces and others.

ii. Helping with weaving, farming, handicrafts training, etc.

iii. Organizing workshops, seminars, meetings, consultations, and awareness programs on various issues.

iv. Research, documentation and GI tags for traditional products

v. Advocacy on AFSPA, 1958.

Brief account of past and present activities of TSL on Human Rights Violation

After independence, many underground groups emerged, particularly in Manipur and Nagaland and many instances of clashes between the underground outfits and the Indian Armed Forces happened, which resulted in torture and ill-treatment of civilians by the Armed Forces. Tangkhul Shanao Long did not remain silent and acted as an intermediary between the Armed Forces and the underground outfits to maintain peace and harmony in the district.

Tangkhul Shanao Long protected the community in many incidents from the angry Armed Forces and fought for the promotion of human rights of the Tangkhul community. They did not confine their work only to human rights movement but also involved themselves in socio-political issues and the peace process of the Tangkhul community.

1. The Tangkhul women's involvement in the human rights movement started in 1974 after the rape incident of Ms. Rose Ningshen, which also gave rise to "East District Women Association" (EDWA). In this incident, the villagers were grouped together and separated into men and women. After being separated from men, many girls and women were raped, manhandled, and sexually abused by the Armed Forces. Villagers were restricted from coming out of the grouping and their houses were raided, valuable things were also robbed.

Tangkhul Shanao Long took the initiative for the immediate arrest and severe punishment of the BSF officers who were involved in the rape of Ms. Rose Ningshen. They organized a rally to protest against the inhuman act committed by the BSF. Shanao Long representative also met with the District Commissioner (DC) Shri Y. Radhysham Singh and strongly appealed to immediately arrest the culprit and to ensure that necessary punishment is given. Shanao Long took the courage to file a case against the BSF officers who were involved in the rape incident and they also submitted a memorandum to the Prime Minister of India, Mrs. Indira Gandhi, on 10th May 1974, demanding befitting punishment to be given to the culprit and for Parliamentary inquiry or judicial inquiry. As a result, with the initiative of Shanao Long, the culprit was court-martialled and a case was opened up in the Civil Court of Imphal for the incident that happened in Ngaprum (Kumram) village.

2. When Ms. Luingamla Muinao from Ngainga village, who was 17 years of age at the time, resisted a rape attempt, she was shot dead by Capt. Mandhir Singh and Lt. Sanjeev Dubey of 25 Madras Regiment on January 24, 1986. Tangkhul Shanao Long organized a mass rally at Imphal as a protest against the killing of Ms. Luingamla Muinao. The rally was attended by MACHA LEIMA, MUTSU, AMSU, NUPILAL, MARUP, NWHL, ATSUM, TUS, TNL, TBL, NSF, NPMHR, and Manipur Tribal Human Rights. They fought the case in the Supreme Court and the convicts were later court-martialled.

3. In the year 1982, the 21st Sikh Regiment committed inhuman acts like molestation, torture, sodomy, rape, forced labor. When they kidnapped and murdered C. Daniel and C. Paul, Shanao Long President and Secretary took the initiative and went for a spot inquiry. They jointly filed a case along with other CSOs against the 21st Sikh Regiment in Guwahati High Court. When the case was registered in the Supreme Court, Tangkhul Shanao Long took great initiative in the case and even requested for intervention of the Government of India by sending a fact-finding team from 17th August till 22nd August 1982. On accepting their request, Tangkhul Shanao Long supported the fact-finding team coming from Delhi initiated by Mr. Luingam Luithui and Mr. H. Sabastian Muisang by providing financial and moral support.

4. In 1986, another fact-finding team was appointed and sent by the Government of India through the initiatives of the Tangkhul Shanao Long for the continuous atrocities committed by the Indian Armed Forces.

5. Tangkhul Shanao Long filed a case against the Assam rifles when they later committed atrocities against women on 15th August 1993, by cross-firing randomly and injuring hundreds of women in Ukhrul town.

6. On May 9th, 1994, when the Assam Rifles killed Mrs. Mathotla (a widow) in her shop with two other people in Ukhrul town, TSL filed a case against the Assam Rifles in the High Court for killing civilians. TSL also accused the Assam Rifles of blowing up 2-inch mortars at residential areas, damaging several houses and properties, injuring many civilians, harassing and torturing hundreds of people, looting valuables, etc.

7. TSL also accused the 20 Assam Riffles of killing Ms. H. Wonchungla, a teenage school girl of VI standard and Mahai (Butcher) on 17th August 1994. The case was later filed in court with the intervention of TSL. Other than such activities, TSL has taken great initiative in the human rights movement.

Future aspiration of TSL:

Tangkhul Shanao Long is looking forward to growing into a bigger and more well-equipped organization that can become self-sufficient in every aspect of life. TSL wants to be fully equipped so that the organization can be self-reliant in its own autonomy. This would help and encourage all women to stand up on their own feet for equal Human Rights opportunities as rightful citizens of the land, both in the family and in society. TSL is exploring the right channels to provide better services, funds, and other resources for the welfare of Tangkhul women. To protect and preserve the cultural identity TSL is engaging in research and documentation. Looking forward to the Publication of Shanvai Chonvai (Traditional Attires) by 2024, the documentary on Phakhreila/ Pukreila by 2024, and the GI (Geographical Indication) tag on Luirim Kachon and others.

Tangkhul Katamnao Saklong (TKS) intervention on Human Rights Violation.[40]

TKS is the biggest apex body of Tangkhul Student Union, also known as Tangkhul Katamnao Saklong (Tangkhul Student Union). TKS is one of the youth organizations and the oldest student union in the state working for the welfare of the society for decades. The history of Tangkhul student union can be traced back to the foundation initiated by William Pettigrew, an American Baptist missionary. He laid the foundation of education in Ukhrul district and first started a Middle English school in February 1897. In 1903, he took a total of 57 boys and made them enroll in elementary school. He selflessly served in the educational field without a break till his stay in the district in 1919.

R. Khathing from Ukhrul, a college-going student, initiated the idea of student conferences with the idea of educational advancement, cooperation with each other, and development in all walks of life. Through his initiative, the first student conference assembly was held in Ukhrul Mission School on

---

[40] Historical Souvenir, Tangkhul Katamnao Saklong 1932-2007

15th June 1932 with the student representative from Nambisha, Ningchou, Bungpa, Apong, Shangshak, Nungshong, Hungbum, Phalee, Shongran, Talui, Lunghar, and Chingjui. The conference was under the assistance and supervision of NG. Ragui and L. Sopei. After the foundation of the Tangkhul Student Conference, R. Khathing was elected as the first president of the Tangkhul Student Conference with an aim toward progressive development in the field of education and overall development. Since the formation of the Tangkhul Student Conference in 1932, they have been involved in defending human rights violations and working for the Human Rights Movement in the district.

Initiatives on human rights violation

1. Rose Ningshen - a rape case:

In the year 1974, a memorandum relating to the case of Rose Ningshen, a rape victim, Ngaprum village (Kumram), Grihang village, was submitted to 95 BSF Bn. on 18th May. TSC submitted another memorandum to the Chief Minister on the construction of the Youth Hostel and District Library.

Through the strenuous pursuit of TSC, the Government favored Ukhrul District by raising the Primary Health Centre to the status of the present District Hospital. TSC was later changed to TKS (Tangkhul Katamnao Saklong) Tangkhul Student Union in 1979.

2. Intervene on enforced disappearance:

The attack of Namthilok by NSCN (IM) on 19th February 1982 resulted in the killing of 21st Sikh Regiment Soldiers and the seizure of arms. As a consequence of the incident, civilians of the village were harassed by the Sikh Regiment, resulting in the kidnap and murder of C. Paul and C. Daniel, where their bodies remained untraced. The movements of the villagers were even threatened, fearing to go to their farm and paddy field.

During this dark period of time, the Journalist Association visited four villages that were living in terror. TKS assisted the visiting Journalist association members namely the Naga People's Movement of Human Rights (NPMHR) and the representatives of Naga Student Union Shillong (NSUS) as the fact-finding team. TKS visited several villages, taking affidavits written and certified exclusively by ZV. Vakham, Advocate. In connection with the atrocities meted out to the villages, NPMHR sued a case against the Sikh Regiment in the Supreme Court. To a certain extent, TKS shared the responsibility with the NPMHR to rescue the affected villages. TKS organized a peace procession twice at Ukhrul which went unnoticed, thus followed by bandhs and economic blockade, in which 150 TKS volunteers were arrested by the 20th Assam Rifles, and some of the volunteers were beaten badly.

3. Advocacy:

During the harassment of the civilians by the Armed Forces, in the midst of which was the brutal killing of Esau of Champhung Changta by the 12th Garhwal Rifles in October 1984 at Talui camp. Many such cases were the order of the day in the pre-cease fire period in which TKS did not remain a silent spectator but was fighting to the greatest extent possible in suing the culprits and getting justice for the victims. In 1986, having failed in an attempt to rape Ms. Luingamla Muinao of Ngainga village, she was later shot dead by Captain Mandhir Singh and Lieutenant Dubey. To get justice, TKS along with Human Rights Activist jointly filed a case against the two army officers, and Captain Mandhir Singh was later court-martialed.

Cases related to the killing of Z.V. Ngachonmi of Sirarakhong village on 24th April 1986 by the 4th Assam Rifles and of R.V. Thomas of Luireishimphung village and Paul of Theiva village by 6th Dogra Regiment and also of E.P. Vincent of East Tusom in January 1986 by 9th Grenadier were filed by TKS in the Court. Subsequently, the 9th Grenadier was replaced by the 8th Kumoan Regiment.

4. Organize peace rally:

The biggest rally ever organized was staged at the district headquarters, organized by TKS in 1994 as a direct condemnation of the uncalled action of the Assam Rifles, who bombarded the Ukhrul district headquarters as retaliation against the gunning down of their major, Major Pakshi and Captain Labsingh by the NSCN (IM). In 1995, the Assam Rifles gunned down three innocent school-going children intentionally at Theiva village after a severe clash between NSCN (IM) and the 25th Assam Rifles. TKS visited the village and collected detailed reports of the incident. TKS strongly condemned and immediately exposed the inhuman and cowardly act of the Assam Rifles to the outside world. In the aftermath of the exposure, the president of TKS and his colleagues were targeted and allegedly charged with working with the NSCN (IM), giving a hard time to the student leaders and the community.

5. Involvement in Nation-building:

The Tenure from 1994 to 1996 under the Presidentship of Standhope Varah saw TKS's active involvement in Nation-building. In the year 1996, when Huishu village was blazed to ashes in the aftermath of the NSCN (IM) and Assam Rifle clash, TKS was the first civil society organization of the district to visit the said village and intervene in the unwarranted army atrocities meted out to the innocent villagers by the Assam Rifles.

6. Confrontation:

Confrontation between the student leaders and the Indian Army was the regular order of the day. The relationship between the Assam Rifles and TKS was at its wit's end. Though the Indian Army gave TKS a hard time, TKS tackled all the challenges that came their way amicably and carried out all its duties smoothly. To let peace prevail, in the year 1996, TKS took an active role in the "Seminar on Peace" in Delhi, organized and sponsored by the Naga Students Federation (NSF) and Shri Kuldip Nayar, making it a grand success. The seminar had its poignant significance as there was no Indo-Naga ceasefire back then.

7. Initiating peace talk:

When the ceasefire between the GOI and NSCN (IM) was signed in the year 1997, TKS openly welcomed the unique development and lauded both parties for the tremendous achievement. During the peace process, TKS took the initiative in mobilizing and campaigning with the general public to support the peace talks.

NPMHR intervention in Human Rights Violation[41]

Naga People's Movement for Human Rights (NPMHR) dealt with Human rights-related issues. They tackled the entire human rights violation problem in Naga-inhabited areas of the Northeast. Since the imposition of AFSP Act, NPMHR has been strongly opposing the Act and insisted on the Central Government repealing the Act from the Naga inhabited areas. NPMHR gave support to the victims to fight back for their rights; there are several

---

[41] http://www.radioradicale.it/exagora/naga-peoples-movement-for-human-rights

incidences in which the Armed Forces committed several crimes and got off scot-free by the government. NPMHR has been a great movement working for the welfare of the community by giving legal assistance to the victims and the community as a whole.

Since the inception of NPMHR, it has consistently strived to bring attention to the human rights violations faced by the Naga community among the Indian population. Keeping in mind the objectives of the organization, the NPMHR activists carried out an intensive study tour of almost all the villages right away. The NPMHR activists were given a warm welcome by all the villages they visited. Discussions and public meetings were conducted where people expressed their strong resentment against AFSPA and the amount of human rights violations they had suffered. On 15th December 1978, the NPMHR activists were joined by the prominent elders and several social activists at Kohima, where they held a huge mass rally. As a response to the existing situation and the bitter experiences of the past many years, the rally collectively passed the following resolutions:

1. Immediate withdrawal of Armed Forces from all the Naga inhabited areas;

2. Including all the Black Laws;

(i) Assam Maintenance of Public Order (Autonomous District) Act, 1952.

(ii) Nagaland Security Regulation, 1962.

(iii) Armed Forces Special Power Act, 1972 to withdraw immediately.

3. Condemn Mr. Morarji Desai's statement "exterminate the (hostile) Nagas and I will not have any compunction in it;"

4. Accuse and condemn the atrocities committed towards the Naga community by the Armed Forces in the past.

5. Condemn the Nagaland state Government for preventing peace rally-procession by declaring "Section 8 of Assam Maintenance of Public Order Act, 1953" upon the entire Kohima Town for one month to disrupt the rally organized by NPMHR at Kohima on 15th December 1978.

Activities:

➢ **Public Campaign:**

NPMHR and its supporters put up a constant movement for the re-establishment of the rule of law to strengthen the movement, and to spread such awareness, NPMHR makes contact with civil human rights organizations and human rights organizations across India. The all-women's fact-finding team that visited Ukhrul district in 1982 strongly condemned the Armed Forces for violating the human rights of the Tangkhul community. There was an exchange of views and experiences between the Nagas and the Indian human rights activists in the 1985 Human Rights Conference organized by NPMHR. Several Christian workers from the southern part of India, Tamil Nadu and Kerala, Human Rights Activists from two northern states, Bihar and Punjab, jointly came together and discussed with the Naga leaders on various issues and aspects of Democratic rights violated by the Indian Armed Forces in the Naga inhabited areas.

> **Public Interest Litigation:**

a) In April 1982, NPMHR wrote to the Supreme Court regarding the violation of human rights committed by the Indian Armed Forces, demanding the legality of PUDR with an intervening Writ Petition challenging the constitutionality of the said Act, 1983, and another NPMHR Writ Petition "Sebastian M. Hongray vs. Union of India."

b) In 1987, NPMHR filed a Writ Petition with the Guwahati High Court, seeking a fair judgment and the necessary penalty, as per the law, for those found guilty of having committed atrocities during the time of Operation Bluebird in the villages.

> **COCOI:**

Operation Bluebird resulted in a massive proliferation of human rights violations in the Naga villages. Due to this, NPMHR alone couldn't gather all the documents to process the case. So they collected affidavits of the victims and raised funds to rehabilitate the victims. Looking at the situation, in October 1987, the Coordinating Committee on Oinam Issue (COCOI) was formed after a meeting organized by various social organizations like NPMHR, the United Naga Council, Manipur, All Naga Students Association, Manipur (ANSAM), and Manipur Baptist Convention Women's Union (MBCWU).

18

HYPOTHESIS TESTING

The following hypotheses have been tested with the use of SPSS and its findings have been presented accordingly. For the Research study, the following hypothesis has been proposed.

Hypothesis-1 (H1): Violation of Human Rights leads to poor living conditions in the Tangkhul community.

Hypothesis - 1 (Table no. H1)

Association between Responsible Factors in Human Rights Violation and Monthly Income.

Responsible factors in Human Rights Violation	Monthly Income						Total
	below 10000	10000 to 20000	above 20000 to 30000	above 30000 to 40000	above 40000 to 50000	above 50000	
Indian Military	26	50	18	4	10	9	117
	31.0%	29.1%	36.0%	20.0%	29.4%	29.0%	29.9%
Insurgents/Unidentified persons	22	55	13	4	12	15	121
	26.2%	32.0%	26.0%	20.0%	35.3%	48.4%	30.9%
State Police Commando and others	36	67	19	12	12	7	153
	42.9%	39.0%	38.0%	60.0%	35.3%	22.6%	39.1%
Total	84	172	50	20	34	31	391
	100%	100%	100%	100%	100%	100%	100%
Pearson's Chi-Square value p = 5.98							

The table indicates the association between the responsible factors in Human rights violations and the Monthly income of the respondents. The responsible factors are categorized into three groups, namely Indian Military, Insurgents/Unidentified persons, and State Police Commando and others.

Association between violation of Human Rights and poor living conditions.

To assess the association between the violation of Human Rights and poor living conditions, Chi-Square Test was administered. The results showed that the association between the two variables namely, Human Rights violations and poor living conditions of the Tangkhul community are not statistically significant (p=5.98).

The factors responsible for the violation of Human rights affected the level of Monthly income of the Tangkhul community. Hence, it is closely related to variables such as economic empowerment, social status, etc. Table no. H1 reveals that due to the Indian Military force, Human Rights are violated, which affects the monthly income of the Tangkhul community of the respondents 117 (29.9%), due to Insurgent's intervention in Human rights violation 121 (30.9%) respondents' monthly incomes are affected, and the monthly incomes of majority 153 (39.1%) respondents are affected due to State Police Commando and others Human rights violation.

It is observed that nearly half (153 or 39.1%) of the respondents said that their monthly incomes were affected due to Human rights violations by the State Police Commando and others. It is clearly seen that there's an association between the violation of Human rights and the monthly income of the respondents as reflected in their economic condition, living conditions, and social status.

Hence, the alternative Hypothesis (H1) of the study that Violation of Human Rights leads to poor living conditions in the Tangkhul community is rejected and is not significantly associated as per the test result.

Though there is a negative association between the violation of human rights and poor living conditions, it is found that due to Human rights violations, curfews and bandh are often imposed and people are restrained from stepping out of their houses for agricultural work, labor work, and office work. It is also found that illegal taxes are also collected by unidentified/unauthorized persons, which also contributes to it.

Hypothesis-2 (H2): Terrorism affects the Socio-economic condition of the Tangkhul community.

Hypothesis - 2 (Table No. H2)

Association between causes of Terrorism activities and Areas affected by Terrorism

Causes of Terrorism activities	Areas affected by Terrorism				Total
	Education	Economy	Religion	Society	
Due to AFSPA	10	10	2	39	61
	18.2%	18.2%	4.2%	16.7%	15.6%
Misuse of powers	37	34	35	159	265
	67.3%	61.8%	72.9%	68.2%	67.8%
Suppressing the Insurgency	8	9	11	34	62
	14.5%	16.4%	22.9%	14.6%	15.9%
Other reason	0	2	0	1	3
	.0%	3.6%	.0%	.4%	.8%
Total	55	55	48	233	391
	100.0%	100.0%	100.0%	100.0%	100.0%
Pearson's Chi-Square value p = 0.37					

The above table indicates the association between Terrorism and Socio-economic condition of the respondents. The causes of terrorist activities have been categorized into four groups, namely: AFSPA, Misuse of power, suppressing the insurgents, and other reasons.

Association between Terrorism and Socio-economic Condition.

To assess the association between terrorism and Socio-economic condition of the respondents, the Chi-Square Test was administered. The results showed that the association between the two variables, namely terrorism and Socio-economic are statistically significant (p=0.37).

Due to terrorist activities, the Socio-economic conditions of the Tangkhul community have been affected. Therefore, it is closely related to the variables such as the living standard, Socio-economic status, etc. Table no. H2 reveals that 61 (15.6%) respondents had their Socio-economic condition affected due to AFSPA. The majority, 265 (67.8%) respondents had their education, economy, religion, and society affected due to the misuse of power by the insurgents, while 62 (15.9%) respondents saw that their socio-economic condition worsened due to oppressive insurgency, 3 (0.8%) respondents were affected in their Socio-economic condition due to other reasons.

It is seen that the majority 265 (67.8%) respondents had their education, economy, religion, and society affected due to the misuse of power by the insurgents. It clearly shows that the association between Terrorism and Socio-economic condition of the Tangkhul community is reflected in their economic condition and social status.

Hence, the alternative Hypothesis (H2) of the study that terrorism affects the Socio-economic condition of the Tangkhul community is accepted and significantly associated with the test result.

Hypothesis-3 (H3): Human rights will bring Peace and Security to the Tangkhul community

Hypothesis -3 (Table No. H 3)

Association between Effectiveness of Human Rights and Social Peace and Harmony

Effectiveness of Human Rights	AFSPA is a threat to social peace and harmony		Total
	Threat	Not a threat	
Effective	71	18	89
	23.5%	20.2%	22.8%
Not effective	75	28	103
	24.8%	31.5%	26.3%
No knowledge	156	43	199

		51.7%	48.3%	50.9%
Total		302	89	391
		100.0%	100.0%	100.0%
Pearson's Chi-Square value p = 20.26					

The table indicates the association between Human Rights and Social peace and harmony of the respondents. The effectiveness of Human Rights has been categorized into three groups namely, Effective, Not effective, and No knowledge.

Association between Human Rights and Social Peace and Security

To assess the association between Human Rights and Social Peace and Security of the respondents, the Chi-Square Test was administered. The results show that the association between the two variables, namely Human Rights and Social Peace and Harmony is not statistically significant (p=20.26).

The Effectiveness of Human Rights shows the level of social peace and harmony in the Tangkhul community. Therefore, it is closely related to variables such as peace, security, safety, etc. Table no. H 3 reveals that 89 (22.8%) respondents are of the view that Human rights are not effective based on social peace and harmony, 103 (26.3%) respondents are of the view that Human rights are not effective on the basis of social peace and harmony, and the majority 199 (50.9%) respondents did not have any knowledge regarding the effectiveness of Human rights.

It concludes that the majority 199 (50.9%) respondents did not have any knowledge regarding the effectiveness of Human rights with reference to social peace and harmony. This clearly shows the association between Human Rights and threats, which reflects on social peace, security, and safety.

Hence, the alternative Hypothesis (H3) of the study that Human Rights will bring Peace and Security to the Tangkhul community is rejected and is not significantly associated.

The negative association can be due to the protracted Naga political issues to which Nagas long for a respectable and permanent solution based on the unique history that the Central Government vehemently denied. This has escalated conflict between the Armed forces and the Naga Insurgents.

19

CASE STUDY

Case study method was applied and the individual cases were presented accordingly.

The following case studies were conducted:

Ø Rape case incident of Rose Ningshen:

Referral: The case study was suggested by elders, human rights activists, and the researcher's curiosity regarding the rape case, which is the first of its kind in the state.

Background of the case:

Ms. Rose Ningshen, a 21-year-old high school student belonging to the Tangkhul tribe hailing from Kumram village, was tragically raped by officers of the 9th Battalion BSF in the house of Mr. R. Khasung on 3rd March 1974, leading to her eventual suicide due to the unbearable shame, frustration, and helplessness that this act of inhumanity caused. This rape incident stands as one of the most infamous human rights violations in the state.

Interaction with Mrs. Ngalawon (Kumram):

The researcher interacted with Mrs. Ngalawon from Kumram, who was in the village when the fateful incident occurred. According to Mrs. Ngalawon, Ms. Rose Ningshen was allegedly raped by the 9th Battalion BSF officers who were posted in her village. Ms. Rose Ningshen and some of the other women had been selected by the Army officers to help them in preparing food. The incident occurred when the other girls had gone out to collect bedding materials.

Being an innocent village girl, the pain and ignominy that Ms. Rose endured were too much for her to bear, ultimately leading to her taking her own life. During that time, Ms. Rose Ningshen was in a relationship with Mr. Stone from Bungpa village, who was then studying in Shillong. When the incident occurred, Mr. Stone was in Shillong and so was unable to attend Ms. Rose's funeral. The final words she left for her beloved boyfriend, Mr. Stone, were a lengthy, heart-touching, and melancholic farewell letter.

Interaction with Ms. Rose's family:

The researcher visited Lt. Ms. Rose's grave site and interacted with her family members on 13th October 2021. Ms. Rose's elder brother, Ngasoring Ningshen, lamented about the fateful tragic incident that had befallen his dear sister. With much regret, he shared that neither the State government nor the Central government took the issue seriously and no monetary compensation was given for the crime committed, and sadly, justice was still being denied for his sister.

Interaction with Mr. Stone's nephew:

Mr. Stone's nephew shared that his uncle's love for Ms. Rose Ningshen is unconditional and that the fateful incident has never been erased from his mind to this day. He always expresses his love and concern for the family of Ms. Rose by helping them in their times of need.

Interaction with Mr. Stone (Ms. Rose's boyfriend):

With deep regret, Mr. Stone recalled the incident that had befallen his loved one, expressing his sorrow and hopelessness about the tragedy that had profusely hurt him and for which justice had not yet been served to date. He also expressed his deep sense of regret for his absence when the incident occurred, and shared that the Investigation Officer had taken the letter which Ms. Rose had left for him, to keep as evidence of the incident and for further investigation.

Interaction with Ateophy Cithung:

As a tribute to Ms. Rose Ningshen, Atophi Chithung designed a beautiful woolen Phanek/Makhela known as Rose Kashan to commemorate her for preserving women's dignity.

While interacting, she lamented that over time, the pattern and design of the Rose Kashan have been customized, diminishing its authenticity. However, she has preserved the original design for herself, ensuring that its originality and uniqueness can be passed on to the younger generation.

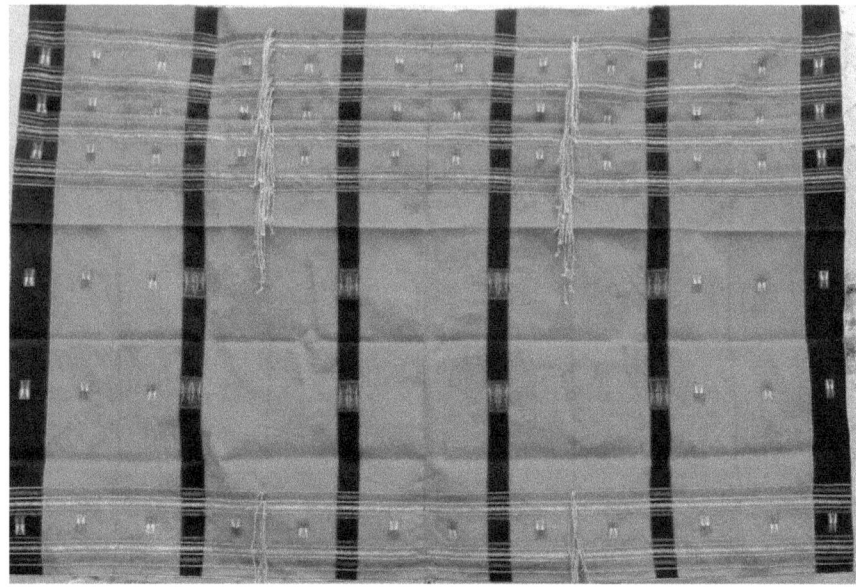

Rose Kashan designed by Ateophy Chithung

Suicide note of Ms. Rose:

The address of the suicide note was made to her brother Angam, saying "In this world filled with sin, my existence is shameful and disgraceful for our family. Today is my last day and nobody can save me. When Amei (Mr. Stone) returns home, tell him about the incident. Justice will never be delivered as they (officers) will get away with it. My brother, do not cry, tell the same to mom, dad, brothers, and sisters that we shall all meet in heaven."

The suicide note was translated into Manipuri, and it was published in a publication of the Pan Manipur Youth League in 1993. The Manipuri version of the note was again translated into English by Ms. R.K Smejita.

The English translation of the letter is as follows:

Most beloved…[42]

---

[42] www.angelfire.com/mi/Nagalim/cont7.htmls,—A Timeless Love letter‖ written by a Tangkhul Rapevictim (A publication of the Pan Manipur YouthLeague in 1993 – Translated to English) Source: AFSPA 1958,CPDM 2010

In a world seeded with envy, our love shall never bloom together like those lovely flowers on the same stalk but we will bloom radiantly in that pure everlasting place of our true love. That I am leaving this world should not bereave you to utter melancholy. A life driven by a gale of sorrow and unrequited words mortifies my soul and leaves me to choose only this lonely path. For the days to come, we made promises to be one and together in our lifelong journey. But oh! My love I couldn't make it at that moment! Oh! My life none is there to receive your lot. What a pity! Oh! My vanquished soul bears the brunt of bereaved feelings every second, bringing me to the threshold of defeat. Even the tears that flow like an eternal spring have now dried up. Those tears were the only image of my life. I will be remembering the tale of you and me in this looming darkness of hell. From dust to dust, let this body embrace its birthplace; let the earth dissolve my remains. Oh! How enviable for that last glance, to see my image in your eyes one last time, but alas! Fate deceives me at this last hour. I choose my own disgraceful death and lo! I will walk as an outcast forever. My love, when you remember me, turn your eyes to those darkest horizons, for I reside forever in the abyss of darkness. There, you will find me treading all alone with a heavy sigh of regrets in that long darkness.

Love of my life! A feeling of sweet remembrance of those long hearty laughs and sharing each other's woes fills my memory. At the dead of this night, far from here my love, a deep slumber will be taking you to pleasant dreams. My last wish to see your visage shall forever remain unfulfilled as you are far from me… far across these ranges of hills.

For my lovely friends, though I am unable to write each of you a parting letter, I plead with you to bid my friends my last farewell. In this early morning, I am glancing over the distance of your lovely place Bungpa. Remember, my love how I wish to shower all my feelings and love, all I have for you is like a cascade flowing down in your ocean of love. Have you ever received the letter I sent to you on 6th Feb. 1973? What could have happened for not receiving any reply from your side? I have waited long and I am still waiting, but at the moment, life steals away stealthily. Why and how we ever got parted will only be known after you escape from this world. Oh Hell! Oh! Abyss of Darkness! I loathe going to the dark passage. No one shall ever know who betrayed whom. The secret is entombed forever.

The life of a maiden dries up from blooming into a flower and lays in heathen... unadorned, unaccepted, untouched. Only regrets on my part for I am choked with words and I am unable to tell you everything at this moment. What remains of the sad tale, I will narrate to you closely in another lifetime, in another eternity. I will end with this note, my love! The only words that erupt from the truest, the innermost part of me is the saddest part of our parting, the story of our failure to be together again.

Yours Rose

The epitaph on the front of the memorial stone is written: **Beloved friends, "When you go home remember to tell them this: I have sacrificed my life in protest against the excesses of the Indian Military actions perpetrated upon the Naga women that they may live in dignity."**

The other two faces read as:

"Oh! What a nightmare of reality the tragedy that befalls you, made tears run dry and hearts that burn will ever be a memory down to the posterity unnamed. May it take a step forward to your people's rights." Family.

"In your death, you brought the Tangkhul women together to stand up for our rights. In your memory, we reaffirm that no woman should ever go through what you went through." TSL.

"No amount of tributes can equal the sacrifice of late Miss. NS Rose of Kumram village in defense of Naga woman's modesty from the savagery of the Indian Army. The act done in silence shall continue to shine like a lighthouse in the mid-sea." NPMHR.

"Behold Miss Rose of Kumram, blooming in the east. You were the envy of every eye: the topic for every tongue suddenly came the sadistic storm that grinned to see you fallen. But you fell down with the seed of promise that bear fruit hundredfold." Kumram.

Grave of Rose Ningshen

Other findings:

She was laid to rest in the backyard of her home, to stay close to her loved ones. A few days after the incident, the police came to their village to conduct a post-mortem and dig up the buried body of the deceased. The post-mortem report has not yet been disclosed to the family hitherto. Angam, the brother of Ms. Rose Ningshen, is also a BSF personnel and to take inquiry, he was taken to the BSF headquarters in Churachandpur district and Pallel (Chandel district). But there was no worthwhile response or outcome from the inquiry. Despite several protests taking place in the state, they went unnoticed. Angam received Rs. 15 as the only financial assistance to meet the travel expenses. This is the only financial assistance given to their family.

Ms. Rose Ningshen's younger sister Azingla said, "My sister did not die of illness; she was raped and committed suicide as she could no longer bear the trauma. The villagers were scared to raise their voices against the security personnel, as they would torture the villagers. Whenever they conducted any operation, they would take the villagers along. We wanted Rose to rest at least in a better place. So the villagers, under the guidance of Tangkhul Shanao Long, contributed money and erected a Memorial Stone at her grave."

The incident became an eye-opener for the Tangkhul women, who realized the urgency and need for the Shanao Long to protect themselves from the predators of women, the Armed Forces. As a result, the East District Women Association (EDWA) was formed on 4th March 1974 to fight against the Armed Forces for the humiliation, inhuman torment, and ill-treatment meted out to the women. Later, the East District Women Association (EDWA) was renamed the Tangkhul Shanao Long (TSL).

Tangkhul Shanao Long took the courage to file a case against the BSF officers who were involved in the rape incident and submitted a memorandum to the Prime Minister of India, Mrs. Indira Gandhi, on 10th May 1974, demanding befitting punishment to be given to the culprit and for Parliamentary inquiry or judicial inquiry. Hence, with the initiative of Shanao Long, the culprit was court-martialed for the crime committed and a case was opened up in the Civil Court of Imphal. Despite this, Ms. Rose Ningshen's family didn't get any compensation from the government and no relief assistance was given to them. Over time, they lost track of the case and were never informed of its progress, eventually, they got disconnected from it. To provide some comfort and consolation to the family after battling for several years for the loss of their loved one, Tangkhul Shanao Long contributed money and erected a Memorial Stone on 6th March 2013 at her grave.

Ø Rape attempt and murder of Ms. Luingamla Muinao:

Referral: The case study was suggested by the human rights activist and the Tangkhul community elders, in addition to the researcher's curiosity about the crime against women.

Background of the case:

The victim was an 18-year-old from Ngainga village who was skilled in weaving and attending a government high school. On the fateful day of 24th January 1986, while she was alone at home, weaving, Capt. Mandhir Singh and Lt. Sanjeev Dubey attempted to rape her, but when she resisted, the two Indian Army officers brutally shot her dead in cold blood.

A huge public meeting was held at Tangkhul Long Ground, Ukhrul along with the dead body of Ms. Luingamla, leading to widespread agitation against her killing. Furthermore, on 11th March, a big rally was held in Imphal which was supported by many valley-based organisations. Consequently, it was resolved that 11th March would thenceforth be observed as the 'Unity Day' of the Hill and Valley people of Manipur. In response, an army court-martial was conducted in 1988, which eventually resulted in the termination from service of Mandhir Singh, who fired the fatal shot.[43]

Interaction with Mr. Wungzak Muinao, elder brother of Ms. Luingamla:

The researcher visited Lt. Ms. Luingamla's graveyard on 10th May 2015 and 4th June 2022 and interacted with the victim's elder brother, Mr. Wungzak Muinao. According to Mr. Wungzak Muinao, Indian Army officers Capt. Mandhir Singh and Lt. Sanjeev Dubey had attempted to rape his sister, but when she resisted, they shot her dead. After killing her, the two went up to the upper side of the locality and falsely informed those who were constructing a house that some insurgents had killed a girl at the lower side of the locality. He, along with his father, were at the construction site, rushed down to their house, and found his sister in a pool of blood flowing from her head. The two Indian Army officers manipulated the entire story in order to escape the accusation. He further shared that the incident was unexpected and the entire village was shocked, and despite several investigations, justice was not delivered.

The State Government provided Rs. 25,000 as ex-gratia compensation after the incident, which they used to cover the expenses of the court case. However, despite their persistent efforts, justice was never delivered. Over

---

[43] https://www.reddit.com/r/IndiaSpeaks/comments/h07hth/attempted_rape_and_murder_of_miss_luingamla/

time, they gave up on fighting for justice due to financial constraints, making it difficult for them to pursue the case further.

With a heavy heart, looking at the dilapidated grave where his beloved sister lies, he implored, "even though my sister has lost the battle, I wish her resting place to be well-maintained, but being poverty-stricken we couldn't afford it."

Grave of Luingamla (Researcher with Mr. Wungzak, Luingamla's brother).

Memorial Stone:

It was only after 25 years that the memorial tombstone was erected and unveiled on 23rd October 2011. The epitaph on the front of the memorial stone is written as:

"Weep no more mummy let the world know I have sacrificed my life in preserving a woman's chastity and dignity blessed by God the creator" showing her courage and dignity to the world.

The other two faces read as:

On 24th January 1986, late Miss Luingamla was weaving all alone. Capt. Mandhir Singh, the then Phungyar Commander of Ngainga,

accompanied by Lieut. Sanjiv Dubey, Mahar Regt. Post Commander of Ngainga, attempted to molest and rape her maiden chastity. As she resisted with all her might and valour, Capt. Mandhir Singh pulled out his pistol and shot her dead in cold blood.'

Our beloved Miss Luingamla Muinao (Maza) we are really proud of your intrepid chastity, your indelible morality, your bold sacrifice be cherished in the Generation to come. Donated by: Ngainga Shanou Long.

Ms. Luingamla's family remained helpless against the Army officers. The graveyard and memorial stone where she was laid to rest looked obsolete and trivial due to financial constraints, making it difficult to maintain. Although many visitors come to see her grave, nobody has ever thought to contribute towards the upkeep of her resting place; they merely come to meet their own purposes.

Luingamla Kashan

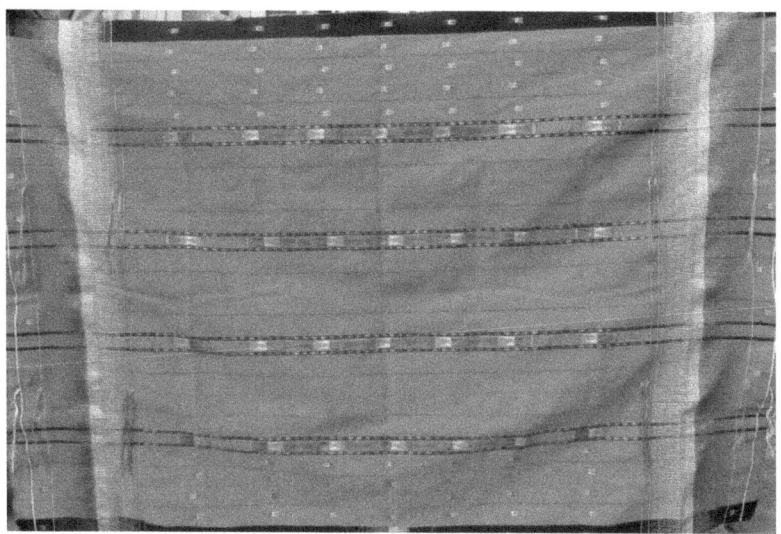

Luingamla Kashan designed by Zamthingla Ruivah

Zamthingla Ruivah, a neighbor of Ms. Luingamla who witnessed the incident, designed a special Phanek/Mekhela known as 'Luingamla Kashan' to eulogize her death and spread a message of women's struggle and bravery. It is interpreted that the 'Luingamla Kashan' was an elegy for a friend in the form of a luminous red Mekhela. The red color signifies

Luingamla's innocent blood that was shed for the cause of women's dignity and honor, reflecting the valor and unflinching courage of women. After four years, some changes were made to the design and pattern.

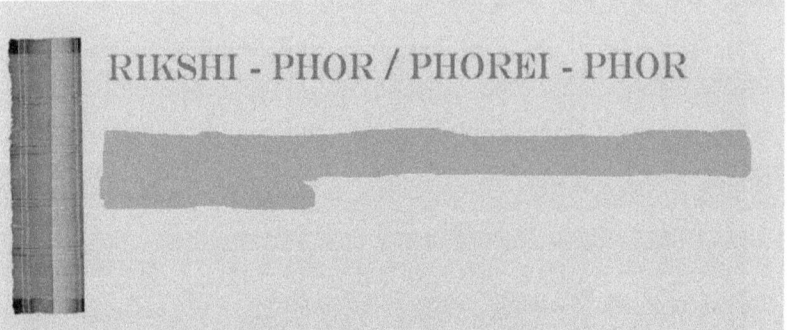

Rikshi-phor/ Phorei-phor

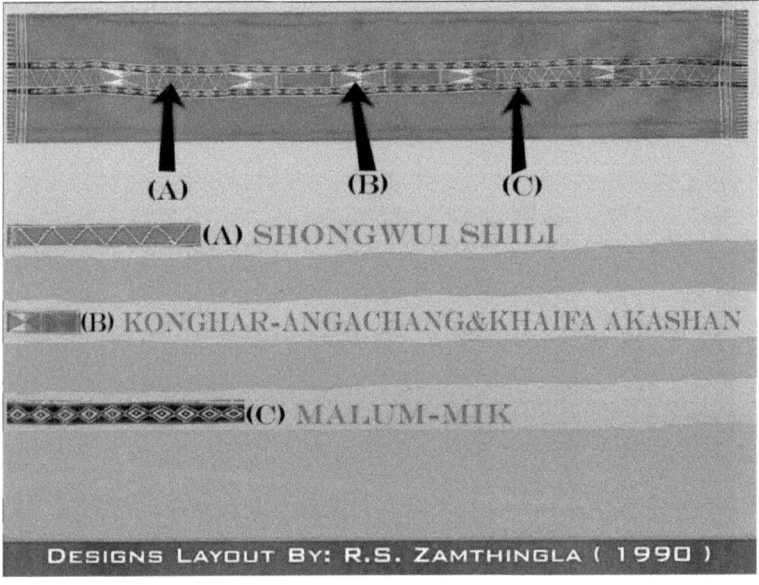

The pattern of a comb and whitish lines symbolize the protection of the chastity of women.

Shongwui Shili

This design where a line of zig-zag indicates how the way for justice from one place to another.

Konghar-angachang/Khaifa akashan

The wings of the butterfly and the waist of the frog's design signify the places of judgment (Courts) firmly for fair justice.

Malum-mik

The two lines in a chain of beads symbolize the eyes of the terminates in a row on the ground, signifying the never-ending support of the Tangkhul women's society and other such organizations, unitedly and relentlessly striving to find the truth until the end of the struggle for justice.

The painful memory continues to linger in everyone's minds in the Tangkhul community. However, Zamthingla's work offers a pathway towards something new through its abstraction, semiotics, and an overturning of the implications of collaboration or the possibilities of political art.[44]

Such a vicious, beastly act should be convicted and a befitting punishment should be given to those who were involved in such a heinous crime. Although the battle seemed to be lost, the collective support for the agitation and the rally organized as a protest from all corners of the state taught the Armed Forces a lesson, ensuring that such crimes are not repeated in Ukhrul district. Thus, it was a victory in the face of defeat.

Ø Enforced disappearance of Mr. Paul, Assistant pastor, and Mr. Daniel, Headmaster of Junior High School of Huining village.

Referral: The case study was suggested by human rights activists, village elders from Huining, and the researcher's curiosity about the enforced disappearance cases.

Background of the case:

On 10th March 1982, Mr. Paul (aged 45) and Mr. Daniel (aged 50), both belonging to the Tangkhul community from Huining village, were picked up by the 21st Sikh Regiment from their village and never returned. Mr. Paul was an assistant pastor of the Huining Baptist Church and Mr. Daniel was the headmaster of the Huining Junior High School.

Interview with Mr. Lt. Vareichin Kasar:

---

[44] Malem Ningthouja's article on Facebook post, 2015

The researcher interacted with Mr. Late Vareichin Kasar, aged 75 (in 2015), who was an eyewitness to the abduction of Mr. Paul and Mr. Daniel by the 21st Sikh Regiment on 10th March 1982. This incident occurred after the 21st Battalion of Sikh Regiment was attacked by insurgents at Namthilok, resulting in the killing of 22 soldiers and the seizure of arms. Following this, the Armed Forces conducted search operations in all the neighboring villages and inflicted torture and beatings on the villagers, irrespective of their age and sex.

The Armed Forces administered electric shocks, took false signatures on paper, and subjected many people to harsh torture, leaving some of them handicapped and emotionally affected. Mr. Paul, an assistant pastor, and Mr. Daniel, the Headmaster, were taken from the village in connection with the incident, and their whereabouts have never been revealed. A missing case was registered, yet justice was not served until long afterward.

Other findings and views:

The People's Union for Democratic Rights (PUFDR), Delhi, filed a case challenging the constitutionality of the Armed Forces Special Power Act 1958. Subsequently, NPMHR activists Mr. Luingam Luithui and Mr. Sebastian Hongray filed a writ of Habeas Corpus on behalf of C. Paul and

C. Daniel on 14 April 1982 (Writ Petition No. 550/82 1993 2 Sec. 109). NPMHR further moved to the Supreme Court of India against Army atrocities and filed a habeas corpus case in the name of another NPMHR member, Sebastian Hongray vs Union of India, Writ Petition {(CRL) No. 148/1983 (1984) 1 SCC, 339}.

Through their initiative, the Supreme Court gave a verdict and imposed a fine of Rs 2 lakh on the culprits for their failure to appear before the court, and granted the families of the two deceased Rs 1 lakh each as compensation for the loss of their family. This was the first time in Indian human rights jurisprudence that compensation was given for excesses committed by the Indian Army. Subsequently, in August 1982, a women's fact-finding team from Delhi representing various organizations from across India was invited to investigate the incident.

This case of enforced disappearance must be unequivocally condemned, and law enforcement agencies must take such cases seriously. The enforced disappearance of Mr. Paul and Mr. Daniel has left their families devastated, as they were the sole breadwinners of their households. Their absence has caused immense distress and suffering for the family, not only emotionally but also financially, leaving them in a vulnerable situation and jeopardizing their future prospects.

Ø Ngainga village arson attack:

Name of the Village: Ngainga Village

Incident year: 1966

Referral: The case study was suggested by human rights activists, Tangkhul community elders, and out of the researcher's curiosity about the village burning incident.

Background of the case:

On 27th February 1966, the Indian Army, along with the Home Guard, fiercely attacked and ousted the NSCN (IM) from the Paosaitarung post, after which they dismantled and burned it down. Following that, the Indian Army vented out their anger by burning down 70 houses in Ngainga village, and in December 1966, without any apparent reason, they burned down the entire village except for 10 houses and the teachers' quarters in order to set up their posts.

Interaction with the victims:

The researcher interacted with the victims and eyewitnesses of the burning incident in Ngainga village. According to them, in February 1966, the Indian Army attacked the Paosaitarung NSCM (IM) post and then vented their anger on Ngainga village, burning down 70 houses. Again in December 1966, they burnt down the entire village except for 10 houses and the teachers' quarters, in order to set up their post. The village headman was beaten up without reason, and as a result, his health deteriorated. Furthermore, many people were also tortured and beaten mercilessly without cause.

The villagers had to seek shelter in the paddy field as their houses had been burnt down. That year, the villagers celebrated Christmas in the paddy field, led by the village pastor. Food, clothes, utensils, and other precious materials had all been burnt down along with their houses; the villagers did not have sufficient food to feed their families. Furthermore, Children could not go to school as their schools had been burnt down and they had to remain at home without schooling for several months. The neighboring villages collected utensils, groceries, clothing, and other needful materials to help rehabilitate the village.

Interaction with Mr. Ashok Y Tipnis, Retd. Captain (aged 85 yrs):

Profile of the client: Mr. Ashok Y Tipnis (Retd. Captain and former Program Director of Volunteers for Village Development (VVD), Ukhrul).

The researcher met Mr. Ashok Y Tipnis (Retd. Army Captain) on two different occasions; on 13th December 2021 and on 7th June 2022 at his residence in Ukhrul. He was the Company Commander leading three Platoons under his command during the Dec 1966 Ngainga incident. On that fateful day, he was only leading two Platoons and had been asked to set up a post at Talui while the other platoon had already been stationed at Ngainga.

Statement by Capt. (Retd) Ashok Y. Tipnis, relating to the Ngainga incident of December 1966.

My Company, of 3 platoons and Coy.-HQ, was commissioned to clear the hostile (Naga Army) post at Ngainga in December 1966. Accordingly, we vacated our posts at Lunghar, Longpi, and Lambui/Ramva, and assembled at Ukhrul.

We carried out the operation, after which my company established a post at Ngainga with one platoon(+). My Coy. HQ + 2 Platoons (-), were placed across the Talui road, at the 'S' road-bend opposite Ngainga village.

Late one afternoon, our post at the road bend was attacked from both directions; from the feature overlooking the post, and from the lower side, from the direction of Posaitarung. The firing was intense and prolonged, and the Ngainga post also came under fire from hostiles, presumably from Talui. At my post, one Senior Havildar and one young Sepoy tragically lost their lives.

While the firing was going on, I saw smoke rising from the direction of Ngainga, and realizing that it was the result of action by our platoon there, I called the platoon commander on the wireless and ordered him to go and put out the fire.

When the hostiles withdrew, I visited the Ngainga post (probably the next day, late evening), my platoon commander explained that his post was attacked from three directions while his water-carrying party was out of the post. In order to ensure their safe return, he had set three unoccupied huts on fire in the direction from which the hostile fire had been coming toward his post.

I do remember that I interacted with the village headman and elders. I remember seeing some partially burned houses. And though I regretted the incident, I had no means to compensate the families.

Soon after this, my Coy. moved out from both locations and occupied a new post at Talui road junction.

Postscript:

I deeply regret the incident, which I remember. My memory of the exact damage to the property is now too blurred.

What I also regret is that having returned to Ukhrul, in 1982, as an NGO worker, and having initiated some project work in Ngainga village, the villagers did not make mention of the incident to me nor did I think about it. If they had, I would have tried to compensate the affected families. Even now, if opportunity offers itself, I would endeavor to help the families financially, in partial atonement of the wrong.

~ Capt. (Retd.)Ashok Y. Tipnis 9th June 2022

Other findings and views:

This incident is utterly reprehensible and does not reflect a constructive approach to problem-solving. Such a cowardly act of arson is completely condemnable and shameful. The entire village was devastated by the blaze, with homes, livelihoods, and precious household materials being utterly destroyed. The entire village was reduced to ashes, and villagers had to take several years and a tremendous amount of effort to rebuild their homes and recover the items that were lost in the blaze.

Despite the village economy being badly affected, the villagers were neither compensated nor provided with any rehabilitation assistance by the government. As such, it is imperative that those responsible for this heinous act are brought to justice and that the affected villagers are provided with the necessary resources to rebuild their lives and recover from their losses. This incident should serve as a reminder of the importance of engaging in constructive dialogue and seeking out peaceful solutions to conflicts, and of the government's responsibility to ensure the safety and well-being of its citizens.

Arson in Ngainga village was accompanied by fiery flames and billowing smoke, incinerating several households to ashes. This event has been deeply ingrained in the memories of the Tangkhul community. Even today, whenever there is an excessive dose of flame and smoke, such as from a cigarette, people often likened it to the arson in Ngainga, saying 'It's like Ngainga's homestead incinerating'.

20

ANALYTICAL FINDINGS

- **Gender**

As per the findings, it is found that 70.6% of the respondents are male and 29.4% respondents are female.

- **Age**

As per the findings, it is observed that 51.2% of the respondents are in the age group of 18-40 years, 39.1% of respondents are in the age group of 41-60, and 9.7% of respondents are 61 years and above.

- **Monthly income**

As per the findings, it is found that 21.5 % of the respondents' families have an income less than Rs 10000, 44.0% of families have a monthly income ranging from Rs 10000 to Rs 50000, and only 7.9% of families have a monthly income above Rs 50000.

- **Type of family**

As per the findings, it is found that 60.6% of the respondents are from the joint family system and 39.4% of respondents are from the nuclear family system.

- **Education**

As per the findings, it is found that 82.4% of the respondents know how to read and write while 17.6% did not know how to read and write. Out of those who can read and write, 79.7% were male respondents and 88.7% were female respondents.

- **Occupation**

As per the findings, it is found that 48.1% of the respondents' families engaged in agriculture 35.0% of families worked in the private sector, and only 16.9% of families worked in the Government sector.

- **Main source of family income**

As per the findings, it is found that 36.6% of the main source of income is generated from Agriculture, 22.5% of the income is generated from private jobs, 21.0% of the income is generated from Government jobs, 19.7% of the income is generated from labor work, and 0.3% of the income is generated from others type of work.

- **Charges for wages**

As per the findings, it is found that 52.2% of the respondents earn Rs. 400 to 500 as their daily wages, 43.0% earn Rs. 501 to Rs. 600 as their daily wages, 4.1% earn Rs. 601 to Rs. 700 as their daily wages, and only 0.8% earn Rs. 700 and above as their daily wages.

The difference in wages for different types of work is due to the workload and level of skill required. Skilled laborers are usually given higher wages due to their expertise and proficiency in their field.

- **NREGA Scheme**

As per the findings, it is found that Almost all the families have availed of the National Rural Employment Guarantee Act Scheme, however, there are a few families who have not.

- **Family category**

As per the findings, it is found that 61.6% of the respondents' families come under BPL category, 27.6% of respondents' families come under APL, and 10.7 % of respondents' families come under AAY.

- **Need for employment**

As per the findings, It is found that many educated youths are jobless and have become underemployed in the private sector, with 95.9% of the respondents found to be in need of employment and 4.1% not necessarily in need of employment.

- **Search for a job outside the district**

As per the findings, it is found that 97.2% of the respondents' families searched for a job opportunity outside the district, with most of the young educated and non-educated youth going to metropolitan cities in search of such opportunities, while 2.8% did not.

- **Shortage of food grains**

As per the findings, it is found that the majority of the families have enough food grains throughout the year. Most of the families cultivate their agricultural land and produce sufficient food grains throughout the year, except for a few families who don't have agricultural land.

- **Socio-economy and livelihood:**

The analytical findings concluded that most of the respondents are from the age group between 18 to 40 years, with a few from 61 years and above. The selected seven villages mostly follow a joint family system and most of the respondents belong to BPL families. On average, the respondents have around 4 to 7 family members with an average monthly income of Rs. 10000 to Rs. 20000 per month.

- **Occupation and food grains:**

More than 50% of the families in the selected villages follow terrace farming and their cropping pattern is usually once a year. There are very few family members employed in the government and public sector and the majority are employed in the private sector with minimal income. Most of the families have sufficient food throughout the year, with Jessami village having the highest number of families with 96.4% having sufficient food throughout the year. The majority of respondents are found to be literate; however, due to the lack of job opportunities, they are compelled to take up subsistence agriculture.

- **Employment and livelihood source:**

There is a need for high employment generation as it is found that many educated youths are unemployed. The Government should be the major stakeholder to accommodate them in various suitable public sectors. It is found that employment opportunities are also generated by the NGOs, Church Ministry, and other private sectors in minuscule and remain wanting to a great extent. Educated youth need to be confined within the district by engaging them in suitable jobs to utilize their skills and potential for holistic development. Moreover, livelihood sources such as pottery, handicrafts, handloom, charcoal burning, firewood cutting, animal husbandry, carpentry, etc., should be encouraged as they immensely contribute to the economy of the Tangkhul community.

- **Racial discrimination:**

It is found that the Tangkhul community experiences racial discrimination from other dominant communities, as well as religious discrimination from non-Christians.

- **Category and Scheme:**

It is found that regarding the socio-economy and living conditions of the Tangkhul community, most of the families belong to the Below Poverty Line (BPL) category. Very few families come under the Above Poverty Line (APL) and Antyodaya Anna Yojana (AAY). Some families have not been able to avail the Government schemes even though they are meant to be available to every poor household.

- **Cultivation and wages:**

For cultivation, terrace farming is done in most parts of the villages due to the geographical location and rugged topography; hence, the production is significantly lower. Only rice is cultivated in the paddy fields, and harvest is only obtained once a year as there is no possibility of double cropping due to unfavorable climatic conditions. Most families depend on subsistence agriculture for their livelihood. The wages are given daily, weekly, and monthly depending on the nature of the work. In the meantime, wages are classified into skilled and unskilled labor. Most agriculture and non-agriculture laborers earn Rs. 400 to Rs. 500 per day as daily wages, while skilled laborers earn more than Rs. 500 per day, depending on the nature of the work and their proficiency.

- **Culture and festivals**

The Tangkhul community has a rich and varied culture, celebrating festivals throughout the seasons one after the other. Luira Phanit (Seed Sowing Festival) is celebrated in almost all the villages of the Tangkhul community. In addition to these traditional festivals, the Shirui Lily Festival (State

Flower Festival) is celebrated annually as a state festival and is one of the most popular festivals in Manipur, second only to the Sangai Festival. Other festivals celebrated by the Tangkhul community include the Lemon Festival at Kachai, Hathei Phanit (Chilli Festival) at Sirarakhong, Banana Festival at Koso, and Shuri Kaso Phanat (Garlic Festival) at Talloi.

- **Violation of human rights and its effect on Socio-economy**

Violation of human rights has had an immense impact on the Tangkhul community. It has resulted in the disruption of the entire social system, leading to inadvertent social problems. It is concluded that the Indian Military, the State Armed Forces, and other unspecified groups have committed gross human rights violations on multiple occasions, thus impeding social and economic growth.

- **Human rights violation and its brutality:**

The leading cause of human rights violations is the implementation of the Armed Forces (Special Powers) Act. While taking advantage of the Act, some Armed Forces personnel have deliberately misused their power, some out of anger and enmity towards the community. Apart from the rights violated, the Armed Forces have committed several crimes advertently; it is recorded that many have been killed, abused, threatened, raped, and sodomized. To mention a few, the rape incident of Ms. Rose Ningshen that resulted in her abetting suicide and the attempted rape and eventual killing of Ms. Luingamla Muinao, and Ngainga village arson are some of these frenzied and heinous incidents that still linger fresh in the memories of the Tangkhul community.

- **Human rights violations and their effect:**

The Indian Army and State Government Forces have used various methods to violate human rights, such as guns, explosive materials, physical force, tear gas, and other harmful objects. Electric shocks, punching, kicking, butt-stroking, and flogging are among the most common punishments inflicted by the Armed Forces. Such violence has created an atmosphere of fear and anxiety, impacting the mental health and psychological well-being of the community.

The Armed Forces have been accused of carrying out human rights violations such as physical assault causing bone fractures, muscle pain, handicaps, deteriorating health conditions, and shortened lifespans. It is reported that curfews, bandhs, body checks, dragging of suspects, kidnapping, open firing at public places, arson attacks, and house raids are often carried out arbitrarily with hostility. Such violations are done without prior notification or warrant, and the victims are rarely compensated for their losses and damages.

- **Human Rights Law:**

Most of the respondents are aware of Human Rights Law and have filed complaints to the police station, but justice has not been delivered most of the time. The Armed Forces have not taken into consideration the sentiments of the community, and have often arbitrarily chosen village leaders for interrogation. As a result, the village youths and village councils suffer the most from harassment and torture.

- **Women and Armed Forces:**

Women are not spared from human rights violations; many times, they are subjected to molestation and manhandling by the Indian Armed Forces. In 1974, the Border Security Force (BSF) resorted to mass rape at Grihang village, the rape incident of Ms. Rose Ningshen resulted in her committing suicide due to ignominy, and an attempt to rape and murder Ms. Luingamla. The State government has not taken enough initiative to look into all these grave cases. The central government too has been a mere spectator in many incidents and justice is delayed hitherto, which means justice is denied.

- **Body search and luggage check:**

It is found that people are not comfortable when they are stopped for a body search by the Armed Forces, as it infringes on their right to privacy. The motives for checking the vehicle may vary, such as looking for insurgents, weapons, suspects, or intoxicants, but the actual action of the search remains intrusive.

- **Christianity and Human rights violation:**

The impious attacks on the church on several occasions have hurt religious sentiments. As a symbol of peace, the church detests instigating violence and terror against innocent people, and in doctrine too, it is totally against biblical principles. Consequently, the church condemns any such violent acts, but it has been made to fall prey to various harsh and uncalled-for reactions from the Armed Forces.

- **Enforcement of AFSP Act:**

The respondents strongly opposed the enforcement of the AFSP Act 1958. By implementing AFSPA, violence has been escalated. Therefore, it is evident that the implementation of AFSPA is not for the safety and security of the community. The civilians have strongly opposed the rules and regulations laid down under AFSPA, and have fought back in response to the violence committed by the Armed Forces. On the other hand, the Armed Forces often override the rules and regulations laid down under AFSPA. This has caused disruption to society, hindered economic growth, and thwarted development. The AFSPA policy has unnecessarily strained human relations and aggravated the politically charged climate in the state. This tense atmosphere has created an intense commotion, and needless to say, has threatened the social peace and harmony of the Tangkhul community, hence it needs to be revoked unconditionally.

- **Terrorism:**

There are many reasons for terrorism, suppressing the insurgency being one of the main ones. According to the opinion of the respondents, terrorism can be reduced if the Armed Forces are evacuated. Terrorist activities, primarily those of the Central and State Forces, have had a profound impact on the lives of many youths, and children have been exposed to the sounds of gunfire and explosions at a very young age, resulting in fear and trauma which can have long-term negative effects on their psychological development. Terrorism has become a threat to the Tangkhul traditional culture, affecting its socio-economic condition, education, and religion. To maintain peace and tranquility, the terrorism issue needs to be addressed judiciously.

It has been a trend that the government appears to be vocally taking the initiative to prevent terrorism, but in reality, is just a mere silent spectator. There is a high degree of indifference from the government to objections raised by the citizens against the perpetrators, including its own agencies. Even when there is strong agitation and protest from civil society organizations, a lackadaisical action is followed, otherwise, it is often ignored. Due to this indifference, most victims prefer not to inform any higher authority in many cases. It is also clear that the promises made to help the victims are often just proposals and lip service. Justice is rarely delivered and most of the time, the higher authority deliberately overlooks justice.

- **Armed Forces and human rights activists:**

It is concluded that the respondents strongly opposed the Armed Forces' attack on innocent civilians. As a remedial measure, peace rallies are often organized to let the media and other parts of the world know about the situation in the district. Women's groups have also raised their concerns and stood up to protest against terrorist activities. In times of violence, police do intervene to control the situation but justice is not always delivered.

Human rights organizations such as the Naga People's Movement for Human Rights are working in the district to restore dignified human rights, yet their efforts are often met with mistreatment and a bad impression from the Armed Forces. Despite their repeated attempts to ensure human rights are respected, they have yet to see a significant change in the attitude of the Armed Forces towards their work.

It is observed that the community is often threatened by the Armed Forces when initiating human rights movements. Moreover, since the Human Rights Commission is not fully functional in Manipur, the influence of the Commission is not seen much in Ukhrul. Nevertheless, Civil Society Organizations and Human Rights Activists play an active role in thwarting the schemes of Central and State-sponsored terrorism.

21

SUGGESTIONS

SUGGESTIONS TO THE ARMED FORCES

- The Armed Forces should not disrupt the social and economic activities of the people. Due to the firing of guns against peaceful protests and strikes, schools, colleges, shops, and businesses are often forced to close. The Armed Forces should be guardians and protectors of the citizens, not adversaries of the social and economic fabric of the community. It is expected that the Armed Forces initiate more welfare services and promote sustainable economic development for the community.

- Arson attacks on villages must never be repeated; such a savage act has caused irreparable losses in the past. As defenders of our nation, they should never commit such a barbaric act, which is tantamount to a heinous crime. The Armed Forces should strive to foster a peaceful environment, promoting mutual respect and peaceful coexistence within the community.

- Human rights violations should not be abrogated or condoned but should be met with appropriate punishment. Too often, the Armed Forces are found to have deliberately committed atrocities with malicious intent, only to be acquitted of any wrongdoing. There are many painful testimonies and traumatic memories of cruel and inhumane wounds inflicted by the Armed Forces, and they must acknowledge and accept responsibility for their actions.

- Armed Forces should initiate a peace process with the community through dialogue and discussion, instead of violence and bloodshed, in order to establish trust and move towards mutually beneficial solutions. They should be open to hearing the issues and concerns of the community, and work towards achieving a peaceful co-existence with the community.

- Safety and security of the citizens should be maintained and respected; many times, such rights are violated, and it is also found that the right to life is denied by the Armed Forces. The right to gather for public discussion and consultation should not be deterred, as people have the right to assemble, in addition to rights to autonomy and self-rule, which are enshrined in the Constitution.

- Rape, killing, sodomy, abuse, threats, extrajudicial killings, etc must be stopped; those committing such inhumane crimes must be held accountable and punished according to the law, with no impunity. All personnel, notwithstanding of military rank or position, must be made aware of the severity of these offenses and the suffering they inflict on communities.

- Armed Forces should not use their power to infringe upon the rights of civilians, as civilians are unarmed and pose no threat. Instead, the military should uphold the rights of civilians and act with respect and responsibility towards the community. The mindset of superiority and authoritarianism must be put to an end in all forms.

- The Armed forces have been illegally occupying Tangkhul villages to set up their camps without the prior consent of the villagers and without providing compensation, thus infringing the special provisions of the 'Right to Fair Compensation and Transparency in Land Acquisition, Rehabilitation and Resettlement Act, 2013 (RFCTLARR Act, 2013) which protects tribals' interests. Such illicit ways of occupation causing distress to the tribals should be ceased.

SUGGESTIONS TO THE GOVERNMENT

- Culprits or perpetrators should not be exonerated regardless of their position or military rank, and the judiciary should take necessary action to ensure justice is served. The concerned authority should be held accountable for any chaos, havoc, and unrest caused by its forces for non-adherence to rules and regulations. It is often seen that the Armed Forces have gone beyond their limits and yet been overlooked; thus, the concerned authority must pay closer attention to such cases.

- Government should take more initiatives to prevent human rights violations. It is the responsibility of the government to look after the needs and address the problems of every citizen, irrespective of their caste, creed, or religion. Government should not remain a silent spectator when citizens suffer and cry out for justice. It should deliver justice and protect the rights of every citizen, regardless of the region or community they belong to.

- The Central and State governments should come to an amicable agreement with the Armed Forces and other non-state actors, and ensure that the cease-fire is respected and adhered to.

- Human rights violation cases reported should be taken seriously by the concerned authorities. The Deputy Commissioner and the Superintendent of Police should promptly investigate such incidents within the district. Any dereliction of duty on the part of the officials should be subject to investigation by a higher authority and sanctioned accordingly. The higher authorities and the Government must comply unwaveringly with International Human Rights Law.

- Government must provide compensation for the loss of lives, damages, and destruction of property. Victims of human rights violations should be immediately rehabilitated without delay.

- The community has been suffering for decades, with numerous cases of human rights violations piling up. The presence of AFSPA in the state has only exacerbated violence and terror, and it is therefore essential that the government review the impact of this law and consider revoking it in order to restore peace and harmony.

- Human rights violations have had a profound effect on the social and religious life of the people of the Tangkhul community, who as Christians, adhere to the spirit of non-violence and peace. Despite this, they have been subjected to incessant aggression from the Armed Forces toward innocent civilians, which has provoked much anger and dismay. As a result, they have been forced to react in violence in response to the continuous attack on their community, which has caused them to inadvertently breach the principles of the biblical teachings of peace and non-violence.

- Impunity should not be granted; rather, it should be scrapped. Exemption from punishment and penalty is unconstitutional and should be stamped out. Such a draconian law should be abolished and felons should be charged with the guilt, up to the extent of even capital punishment or life imprisonment, before the law.

- Those Armed Forces who treat denizens violently should be given immediate transfer, and if necessary, the entire unit should be evacuated to make the Armed Forces more conscious and aware of their duties and the consequences of their actions. High-ranking officers who deliberately commit crimes should be subject to immediate termination from the service and given befitting punishment for their offenses committed.

- The Central and State Governments need to initiate more platforms for discussion and dialogue to address issues of human rights violations. Rather than resorting to forceful suppression, it is important to first understand the perspectives of the insurgents, which can be achieved by engaging them in a peace process through constructive dialogue and negotiation.

- The Government should not be biased in protecting citizens during communal crises and emergencies, irrespective of caste, creed, religion, region, and socio-political differences. Such unfair administration can have a detrimental effect on the community, leading to divisive divisions that would be unhealthy for the Government and could result in adverse reactions against the Government.

SUGGESTIONS TO THE MANIPUR HUMAN RIGHTS COMMISSION

- The non-functional state of the Human Rights Commission in the state for a long time has affected the timely execution of justice and preservation of law and order. To maintain peace and harmony, it is essential that the Manipur Human Rights Commission be fully functional with its full-time chairperson and extended to cover all the hill districts, giving citizens the right to avail protection from the Commission irrespective of region.

- Fake encounters for subterfuge by the Armed forces should be flagged by the path of constitutional justice, including the judiciary, and should be investigated by the State Human Rights Commission. Nobody should be exempted from delivering justice, and the Commission should be vigilant enough to take note of any breaches of legal safeguards and constitutional rights.

The State Government, Central Government, and Human Rights Commission should scrupulously monitor and discourage any human rights violations. They should not turn a blind eye or remain a mute spectator when innocent citizens' lives are threatened and killed under the pretext of a provision of the law underwriting political chicanery. Exploitation based on caste, tribe, region, and religion should be strictly averted; equal treatment should be given irrespective of socio-political differences, and justice must be served for all atrocities. Respecting humanity is the first step to initiating peace, and it is certain that if the Armed Forces make way for humanity, then human rights violations can be quelled. It is the utmost desire of the denizens of Ukhrul that equal respect for citizens should be ensured and that the rule of law should prevail for peaceful co-existence.

KUKNALIM

Victory to our people and land
in their fight against AFSPA

REFERENCES

1. [India] Joint Statement of Women's Groups Against Armed Forces (Special Powers) Act, 1958 (AFSPA).
2. 152 SHRC: 'Social Audit Report-II, Human Rights Violations in Manipur'.
3. Angkang Stephen, Personal Interview, (2013) by Mawon Somingam.
4. Anil Kamboj (2004): 'Strategic Analysis Manipur and Armed Forces (Special Powers) Act 1958,' Strategic Analysis, Vol. 28, No. 4, Oct-Dec 2004.
5. Armed Forces Special Powers Act: The Debate, IDSA Monograph Series, No.7 November 2012. ISBN 978-81-7095-129-1, S. Kumar for Lancer's Books, P O Box 4236, New Delhi-110048. In Association with: Institute for Defence Studies and Analyses No. 1, Development Enclave Rao Tula Ram Marg Delhi Cantt., New Delhi-110010.
6. Attar Chand, "Politics of Human Rights and Civil Liberties - A Global Survey" (Delhi: UDH Publishers, 1985) 45.
7. Baseline Survey of Minority Concentrated Districts, District Report UKHRUL, Study Commissioned by Ministry of Minority Affairs Government of India. Study Conducted by Omeo Kumar Das Institute of Social Change and Development, Guwahati.
8. C.R Kothari (2004): "Research Methodology, Methods and Techniques," second revised edition, New Age International Publishers.
9. ChamanLal, IPS Retd (2004): 'Human Rights Situation in the North-East,' Dialogue April - June, 2004, Volume 5 No. 4.
10. Change.org, Themmarak kapai; "Petitioning Narendra Modi, Hon'ble Prime Minister of India".

11. Cover Photo Credit: Bikash Singh @bikash_ET, Northeast Today & The Economic Times.

12. Declaration of the United Nations signed on January 1, 1942 at Washington, signed by 26 states, including USA, UK, USSR and China.

13. Document - India: Briefing on The Armed Forces (Special Powers) Act, 1958.

14. Document of the American Foreign Relations,(1941) "Declaration by the American President, Franklin D. Roosevelt" on January 6, 1941, Vol. 111, 1941): 26.

15. Dr. Sailajananda Saikia (2014),: 'A Critical Review on Armed Forces Special Power Act (AFSPA), and Human Right Violation in North East India,' Journal of Social Welfare and Human Rights, March 2014, Vol. 2, No. 1, pp. 265-279.

16. Fact Finding Report to the Nation (2009), 'Democracy 'Encountered': Rights' Violations in Manipur Independent Citizens',' November 2009.

17. Gary J. Bass (book reviewer), Samuel Moyn (author of book being reviewed), October 20, 2010, The New Republic, The Old New Thing, Retrieved July 20, 2017.

18. Government of India, "National Commission for Schedule tribes"

19. Historical Souvenir, Tangkhul Katamnao Saklong 1932-2007.

20. H.O. Agarwal (2002), "International Law and Human Rights," 8th ed. (Allahabad: Central Law publications, 2002) 656.

21. H.O. Agarwal, "Human Rights," 7th ed. (Allahabad: Central Law Publications, 2004) 8.

22. http://e-pao.net/epSubPageExtractor.asp?src=education.Human_Rights_Legal.Human_Rights_Issues_And_Participation_Of_Tangkhul_Women_Part_1_By_Maireiwon_Ningshen.

23. http://e-pao.net/GP.asp?src=23..160922.sep22.

24. http://ifsw.org/policies/human-rights-policy/.

25. http://www.kenpro.org/sample-size-determination-using-krejcie-and-morgan-table/.

26. http://www.radioradicale.it/exagora/naga-peoples-movement-for-human-rights
    http://www.sacw.net/Wmov/JointStatement20012005.html.
27. https://indianexpress.com/article/opinion/columns/indian-army-assam-sit-afspa-assam-7968078/.
28. https://kharingyoshimrah01.wordpress.com/2016/04/13/the-social-structure-of-tangkhul-naga/.
29. https://nenow.in/north-east-news/manipur/manipur-villagers-stage-massive-protest-in-ukhrul-against-assam-rifles-demand-afspa-repeal.html.
30. https://thefrontiermanipur.com/hc-pulls-up-manipur-govt-gives-10-days-to-initiate-process-to-appoint-mhrcchief/#:~:text=Khaidem%20Mani%20was%20appointed%20the,or de r%20on%20January%204%2C%202018.
27. https://thefrontiermanipur.com/thousands-attend-rally-against-afspa-forceful-occupation-of-tangkhul-lands-by-assam-rifles/.
28. https://timesofindia.indiatimes.com/the-afspa-and-manipur-10-key-points/listshow/53613784.cms.
29. https://www.eastmojo.com/manipur/2022/09/15/thousands-protest-in-ukhrul-against-assam-rifles-demand-afspa-repeal/.
30. https://www.facebook.com/media/set/?set=a.404432026287751.96106.382340698496884&type=1&l=9df6eca75c.
    https://www.northeasttoday.in/2021/12/27/nagaland-court-of-enquiry-will-be-initiated-against-army-personnel-involved-in-oting-massacre/.
31. Human Rights in Manipur by – Geetanjali Khangembam, E-PAO, Tuesday, Jan 20, 2015.
32. Human rights initiative for indigenous advancement and conflict resolution, Human rights special report Manipur–2009.
33. Indian citizenship regained: "The 22-year ordeal of Luingam Luithui for justice," Edited by Joyjeet Das.
34. Indo-Naga Rairei Wung Regionna ngarara kahai Thotchan. Published by Talui Ex-NNC/FGN Workers' Long 2012.

35. Jawaharlar Nehru. "The Discovery of India, 2"ded. (New Delhl. Jawaharlal Nehru Memorial Fund, 1992) 88.
36. Justice A.M. Ahamadi, "inaugural Address on Fakhruddin Ali Ahamed Memorial Lecture on Democracy." Liberty and Changing Political Scenario, Date 29th July 2000, (New Delhi: GHAL B Institute Publication, 2000) 9.
37. Know your laws: "CrPC, Section 144, 'Prohibition of Assembly'."
38. M. Ningamba Singha, M. Ninghaiba Singha and Th. Kanchanbala Singha: The Status of Human Rights Violations in Manipur, International Journal of Interdisciplinary and Multidisciplinary Studies, 2014, Vol. 1, No. 3, 51-55, ISSN: 2348 – 0343.
39. Maireiwon Ningshen: Human rights issue in Manipur and participation of tangkhul women. Imphal Times, http://www.imphaltimes.com/it-articles/item/6766-human-rights-issues- in-manipur-and-participation-of-tangkhul-women.
40. Major incidents of terrorist violence in Manipur, 1992-2017. http://www.satp.org/satporgtp/countries/india/states/manipur/data_sheets/ majorincidents.htm.
40. Malem Ningthouja article on Facebook post, 2015.
41. Mawon Somingam, Understanding the Origin of the terms 'WUNG', 'HAO' and 'TANGKHUL', Vol. 3(5), 36-40, May (2014), International Research Journal of Social Sciences, ISSN 2319–3565.
42. Naga Army Paosaitarung, 1966. Published by Wung Naga Army, Federal Government of Nagaland (FGN).
43. Naga People Movement for Human rights (NPMHR) pending cases.
44. Nagendra Singh, "Enfor-ement of Human Rights" (Calcutta: Eastern Law House Pvt. Ltd, 1986) 7.
45. Ngainga Shanao Long Silver Jubilee 2012, THOTCHAN, published by History committee Ngainga Shanao Long.
46. Nickel, James,(2017) "Human Rights", The Stanford Encyclopedia of Philosophy, Edward N. Zalta (ed.).
47. P.N. Bhagwati, "Supreme Court of India, Inaugural Address in the Seminar on Human Rights Organised by International Law Association (Allahabad Centre, 1980):7."

48. P.N. Bhagwati, Seminar on Human Rights 7.
49. Revisiting Rape Victim Rose Ningshen 43 Years Later, The Sangai Express, 12 May 2017.
50. S. Radhakrishnan (trans.) "The Bhagavadgita (London: George Allen and Unwin, 1958) 276."
51. Shaw, Malcolm (2008). International Law (6th ed.). Leiden: Cambridge University Press. ISBN 978-0-511-45559-9.
52. Shimreingam A Shishak (2016) The Nagas: Yesterday, today & tomorrow, part-1Chapter-1&2, yesterday & today.
53. Statistical Profile of Scheduled Tribes In India 2013, Ministry Of Tribal Affairs Statistics Division Government Of India. P.2.
54. Status of human rights in Manipur North-eastern region Submitted to the Office of the High Commissioner for Human Rights 28 November 2011.
55. Submission of Committee on Human Rights (COHR), Manipur on human rights situation in Manipur (India) to (COHR).
56. The Armed Forces (Special Powers) Act, 1958 Act No. 28 of 1958, 11th September, 1958.
57. The Armed Forces (Special Powers) Act, 1958 in Manipur and other States of the Northeast of India: Sanctioning repression in violation of India's human rights obligations 18 August 2011.
56. The Asian Centre for Human Rights: An analysis of Armed Forces Special Powers Act, 1958, PUCL Bulletin, March 2005.
57. The Code of Criminal Procedure, 1973 Act no. 2 of 1974, 25th January, 1974https://www.oecd.org/site/adboecdanti-corruptioninitiative/46814340.pdf.
58. The Naga Society, Dr. Chandra Singh (2008) Manas Publication.
59. The Naga Society, Dr. Chandra Singh (2008) Manas Publication.
60. The United Nations, Office of the High Commissioner of Human Rights, What are human rights?, Retrieved July 20, 2017.
61. Ukhrul district profile Government of India.
62. Vibhuti Patel Human Rights Movements in India, Social Change 40(4) 459–477, © CSD 2010 SAGE Publications.

63. Wenona T. Singel, Indian Tribes and Human Rights Accountability, 49 San Diego L. Rev. 567 (2012), Michigan State University College of Law.

64. Yambem Laba, The statement: tale of two ambushes http://webcache.googleusercontent.com/search?q=cache:http://www.the st atesman.com/north/a-tale-of-two-ambushes-70817.html&gws_rd=cr&ei=GqqfWYLwA8bNvgSm_ojoAg.

65. Yogesh K. Tyagi, "Third World Response to Human Rights," Indian Journal of International Law, Vo.21, No.1 (January -March 1981): 120-121.

ABBREVIATIONS

AAY- Antyodaya Anna Yojana

AFSPA- Armed Forces (Special Powers) Acts

AHRC- Asian Human Rights Commission

AMSU - All Manipur Students Union

ANSAM- All Naga Students Association Manipur

ANSUM - All Naga Students Union of Manipur

AR- Assam Rifle

BC- Before Christ

BSF - Border Security Force

Capt.- Captain

CEO- Chief Executive Officer

COHR- Committee on Human Rights

CrPC- Criminal Procedure Code

CRPF- Central Reserve Police Force

DIG - Deputy Inspector General of Police

FACAM- Forum Against Corporatization and Militarization

FIR - First Information Report

GoI- Government of India

Govt.- Government

Hav.- Havildar

HRA - Human Rights Alert

ICCPR - International Covenant on Civil and Political Rights

ICDS- Integrated Child Development Services Scheme.

IPC- Indian Penal Code

IRB- Indian Reserve Battalion

JWP- Joint Women's Programme

KNA- Kuki National Army

KYKL- Kanglei Yawol Kanna Lup

Lt. Col- Lieutenant Colonel

MHRC - Manipur Human Rights Commission

MMS- Mahila Makshita Samiti

MNPF- Manipur National People's Front

MR- Manipur Rifle

NHRC- National Human Rights Commission

NLC - Ngariching Living Centre

NPMHR- Naga People's Movement for Human Rights

NSCN (IM) - National Socialist Council of Nagaland (Isak and Muivah)

NSCN- National Socialist Council of Nagaland

NSF- Naga Student Federation

NSUS- Naga Student Union Shillong

NWUM- Naga Women's Union Manipur

OBC- Other Backward Class

PLA- People's Liberation Army

PREPAK- People's Revolutionary Party of Kangleipak

PTSD - Post Traumatic Stress Disorders

PUDR- People's Union for Democratic Rights

Rtd.- Retired

SAI- Sports Authority of India

SC- Schedule Caste

SDM - Sub-Divisional Magistrate

SF - Security Force

SPSS- Statistical Package for the Social Sciences

ST- Schedule Tribe

TKS- Tangkhul Katamnao Saklong

TMNL- Tangkhul Mayar Ngala Long

TNL- Tangkhul Naga Long

TSC- Tangkhul Student Conference

TSL- Tangkhul Shanao Long

UDHR- Universal Declaration of Human Rights

UDSA- Ukhrul District Sports Association

UG- Under Ground

UN- United Nations

UNHCR- United Nations High Commissioner for Refugees

UNICEF- United Nations International Children's Emergency Fund

UNLF- United National Liberation Front

Appendix

INTERVIEW SCHEDULE

I. PERSONAL INFORMATION

1.1 Name…………………………………………..

1.2 Village……………………………………………

1.3 Gender:

(a) Male

(b) Female

1.4 Age:

(a) Between 18-40

(b) Between 41-60

(c) 61 and above

1.5 Marital status:

(a) Married

(b) Unmarried

1.6 Caste:

(a) ST

(b) SC

(c) OBC

(d) Others

1.7 Occupation:

(a) Farmer

(b) Govt. employee

(c) Private employee

1.8 Education:

(a) Literate

(b) Illiterate

1.9 Religion:

(a) Hindu

(b) Muslim

(c) Christian

(d) Others

1.10   Languages Known:

(a) Hindi

(b) English

(c) Tangkhul

(d) Manipuri

(e) Others

II. FAMILY CONSTELLATION

Sl. No	Name	Age	Sex	Relationship with the Respondent	Marital Status	Education	Occupation

2.1 Monthly income of Family...................

2.2. Total no. of family............................

2.3 Total no. of males...............................

2.4 Total no. of females...........................

2.5 Type of family

(a) Joint

(b) Nuclear

2.6 Did your entire family members stay in the village?

(a) Yes

(b) No

2.7 Are any of your family members employed in the private sector?

(a) Yes

(b) No

2.8 Are any of your family members Government employees?

(a) Yes

(b) No

2.9 Which category does your family come under?

(a) AAY

(b) BPL

(c) APL

2.10　Did your family receive NREGA scheme?

(a) Yes

(b) No

III. Information about the Socio-economic condition of the Tangkhul tribal community.

3.1 Does the Tangkhul community have a good relationship with other tribes of Manipur?

(a) Yes

(b) No

3.2 Does the Tangkhul community face racial discrimination by the dominant Meitei community?

(a) Sometimes

(b) Very often

(c) Not at all

3.3 Does the Tangkhul community face religious discrimination from the non-Christians of Manipur?

(a) Yes

(b) No

3.4 Does the Tangkhul community feel an inferiority complex towards the other tribes of Manipur?

(a) Yes

(b) No

3.5 Do the other communities violate the rights of Tangkhul community?

(a) Yes

(b) No

3.6 What is the main source of income for your family?

(a) Govt. job

(b) Private job

(c) Labor work

(d) Agriculture.

3.7 What is the main occupation in Ukhrul district?

(a) Farming

(b) Business

(c) Govt. job

(d) Private Job.

3.8 How much is your daily wages?

(a) Rs. 400 to 500

(b) Rs. 501 to 600

(c) Rs. 601 to 700

(d) Above Rs. 700

3.9 Which type of labor is prevalent in your village?

(a) Agriculture

(b) Non – Agriculture

3.10 Which type of cultivation is followed in your village?

(a) Jhum cultivation

(b) Water cultivation

(c) Terrace cultivation

3.11 Did you get sufficient food throughout the year?

(a) Yes

(b) No

3.12 Do you feel the need for more employment generation for your community?

(a) Yes

(b) No

3.13 Do religious institutions generate a platform for job opportunities?

(a) Yes

(b) No

3.14 Does the Tangkhul community go out to other districts in search of jobs?

(a) Yes

(b) No

3.15 Apart from Agriculture, which are the other sources of livelihood for your family?

(a) Potter making

(b) Handicraft

(c) Handloom

(d) Charcoal burning

(e) Firewood cutting

IV. Information about the violation of Human rights within the Tangkhul tribal community.

4.1 Who is violating human rights in Ukhrul district?

(a) Central Armed Forces

(b) Unidentified/Unspecified

(c) State police and others.

4.2 Why is the violation happening?

(a) No reason

(b) Due to AFSPA

(c) Exposing power

4.3 Which rights are being violated?

(a) Right to safety and security

(b) Right to protest and gather public opinion

(c) Right to autonomy and self-rule

(d) Right to self-respect

(e) Others

4.4 What types of crimes are committed?

(a) Rape

(b) Killing

(c) Abuse

(d) Physical abuse

(e) Threatening

4.5 What is the purpose of violation?

(a) Out of anger

(b) Hostility

(c) No reason

4.6 Did they violate the rights intentionally?

(a) Yes

(b) No

4.7 Which type of punishment is given by the Armed Forces?

(a) Electric shock

(b) Punching and Kicking

(c) Hitting with gun (Buttstroke)

(d) Beating with stick (Flogging).

4.8 Which of these effects do you feel after human rights violation?

(a) Emotional effect

(b) Mental effect

(c) Physical effect

4.9 Are you aware of human rights law?

(a) Yes

(b) No

4.10 Do you register complaints to the police for violation of your rights?

(a) Yes

(b) No

4.11 What is the method of violation of human rights?

(a) Gun

(b) Explosive material

(c) Physical strength

(d) Tear gas

4.12 What are the effects of physical punishment?

(a) Fracture of bones

(b) Physical pain

(c) Handicap

(d) Health weakening

(e) Shortening of lifespan

4.13 Have you ever been a victim of Human Rights violation?

(a) Yes

(b) No

4.14 Did the government take the initiative to prevent violations?

(a) Yes

(b) No

4.15 Which is the most common violation?

(a) Body check

(b) House raid

(c) Curfew

(d) Dragging the suspect

(e) Kidnapped

(f) Open firing at public places

4.16 Did the Indian Military give a warrant and notification before the violation?

(a) Yes

(b) No

4.17 Did the Armed Forces understand the sentiments of the civilians?

(a) Yes

(b) No

4.18 Who is the most likely sufferer of violation?

(a) Women

(b) Youth

(c) Elders

(d) Village Council

4.19 Is violence the only means to achieve the goal of the Armed Forces?

(a) Yes

(b) No

4.20 Do you feel comfortable if your vehicles are stopped and checked by the Army?

(a) Yes

(b) No

4.21 What is the reason for checking vehicles and houses by the Armed Forces?

(a) Looking for insurgence

(b) Looking for weapons

(c) Looking for a suspect

(d) Looking for Drugs and Intoxicants

4.22 Does the Military provide compensation for any damage done by them?

(a) Yes

(b) No

4.23 Do you feel comfortable when the military conducts a body search and luggage check?

(a) Yes

(b) No

4.24 Do such violations affect the religious ethics of Christianity?

(a) Yes

(b) No

V. Opinion of Tangkhul tribal community towards Armed Forces Special Power Act.

5.1 Do you agree with the enforcement of AFSPA?

(a) Agree

(b) Strongly agree

(c) Disagree

(d) Strongly disagree

5.2 Do you feel AFSPA is implemented for the safety and security of civilians?

(a) Yes

(b) No

5.3 Do the civilians accept the rules and regulations laid down under the AFSPA?

(a) Accept

(b) Strongly Accept

(c) Opposed

(d) Strongly Opposed

5.4 Did violence increase with the imposition of AFSPA?

(a) Yes

(b) No

5.5 Did you fight back against the violence committed by the Indian Military?

(a) Yes

(b) No

5.6 Do you think ASFPA will bring peace and non-violence to the Ukhrul District?

(a) Agree

(b) Strongly agree

(c) Disagree

(d) Strongly disagree

5.7 Did AFSPA reduce the growing numbers of insurgent groups?

(a) Yes

(b) No

5.8 Do you want to appeal to the government to remove AFSPA?

(a) Yes

(b) No

5.9 Did the AFSPA bring good relations between the community and the Armed Forces?

(a) Yes

(b) No

5.10 Did the Military abide by the rules and regulations laid down under AFSPA?

(a) Yes

(b) No

5.11 Do you think that AFSPA is imposed for abolishing Insurgency?

(a) Yes

(b) No

5.12 Do you know that AFSPA is imposed for the safety of civilians?

(a) Yes

(b) No

5.13 If AFSPA is removed, will the relationship between the Military and civilians improve?

(a) Yes

(b) No

5.14 Which negative impact has been brought about due to the enforcement of AFSPA?

(a) Social disorganization

(b) Economic degradation

(c) Religious ethics

(d) Political Crisis

5.15 Is AFSPA a threat to social peace and harmony?

(a) Yes

(b) No

VI. Opinion of Tangkhul tribal community towards Terrorism activities.

6.1 What is the main cause of Terrorism in Ukhrul district?

(a) Due to AFSPA

(b) Misuse of powers

(c) Suppressing the Insurgency

6.2 Will Terrorism be reduced if the Indian Military is evacuated from Ukhrul District?

(a) Yes

(b) No

6.3 Is Terrorism affecting your life?

(a) Yes

(b) No

6.4 Are the children afraid of gun firing?

(a) Yes

(b) No

6.5 Did Terrorism have a psychological effect on the community?

(a) Yes

(b) No

6.6 Do you want terrorism activities to be stopped?

(a) Yes

(b) No

6.7 Do you agree that the Military is violating the right to life?

(a) Agree

(b) Strongly Agree

(c) Disagree

(d) Strongly Disagree

6.8 Did the State government take initiatives to stop terrorism?

(a) Yes

(b) No

6.9 Are you afraid of the Indian Military?

(a) Yes

(b) No

6.10 Did civil organizations take initiatives to stop terrorism?

(a) Yes

(b) No

6.11 Do you agree terrorism is violating Human Rights?

(a) Agree

(b) Strongly Agree

(c) Disagree

(d) Strongly Disagree

6.12 Are Women spared from terrorism?

(a) Yes

(b) No

6.13 Did terrorism affect the religious ethics of Christianity?

(a) Yes

(b) No

6.14 What measures have you taken up to stop terrorism?

(a) Peace rally

(b) Informed the D.C.

(c) Contacted the Human Rights Organisation

6.15 Which areas have the violation of human rights impacted?

(a) Education

(b) Economy

(c) Religion

(d) Society

6.16 Have you ever initiated peace talks and discussions with the Indian Military?

(a) Yes

(b) No

6.17 Do you feel secure residing along with the Indian Military in your locality?

(a) Yes

(b) No

6.18 Do you think terrorism is a threat to Tangkhul Traditional Culture?

(a) Yes

(b) No

6.19 Do you oppose the attack of civilians with explosive materials?

(a) Yes

(b) No

6.20 Did Womenfolk stand up to stop terrorism?

(a) Yes

(b) No

VII. Remedial measures on the prohibition of terrorist activities.

7.1 How can terrorism be reduced?

(a) Removed AFSPA

(b) Respecting Human Rights

(c) Stop Misusing power

(d) Evacuation of Military

7.2 Have you taken any initiative to prohibit violence?

(a) Yes

(b) No

7.3 Did police intervene to prevent violence?

(a) Yes

(b) No

(c) No Knowledge

7.4 Do the Human rights activists have a good connection with the Armed Forces?

(a) Yes

(b) No

7.5 Do the civilians have good relations with the police?

(a) YesNo

7.6 Did the police give a positive response to the complaint about terrorism?

(a) Yes

(b) No

7.7 Does the Military accept its mistakes when destruction happens?

(a) Yes

(b) No

7.8 Did you report the violation of your rights to the Human Rights Office?

(a) Yes

(b) No

7.9 Did the Central Government take initiatives to prevent violation of Human Rights?

(a) Yes

(b) No

7.10 Do you think your cry for justice is in vain?

(a) Yes

(b) No

7.11 Does the Indian Military respect Human Rights?

(a) Yes

(b) No

7.12 Does the Military threaten you when you initiate Human Rights movement?

(a) Yes

(b) No

7.13 Do women's groups join in the Human Rights movement?

(a) Yes

(b) No

7.14 How effective is the Human Rights Commission in Ukhrul District?

(a) Effective

(b) Not Effective

(c) Don't Know

7.15 Do you think Human Rights Movement can stop terrorism?

(a) Yes

(b) No

VIII. Information related to the level and method of social workers' intervention for the prohibition of terrorist activities.

8.1 Have you ever reported to social activists for assistance?

(a) Yes

(b) No

8.2 Do you want social workers to intervene in social crises?

(a) Yes

(b) No

8.3 Do you get good responses from social activists?

(a) Yes

(b) No

8.4 If counseling centers are set up, will it help the community?

(a) Yes

(b) No

8.5 Do you need guidance about Human Rights Laws?

(a) Yes

(b) No

8.6 Do you feel the need for training to equip yourself to defend yourself against violation of rights?

(a) Yes

(b) No

8.7 Do you want NGOs to conduct seminars for Woman empowerment?

(a) Yes

(b) No

8.8 Do you want to collaborate with NGOs to solve violation problems?

(a) Yes

(b) No

8.9 What are your expectations from social workers?

(a) Initiating peace

(b) Giving training

(c) Releasing social tension

(d) Bringing social change

8.10 Do you think the Military will consider social workers' intervention plea for justice?

(a) Yes

(b) No

Photo of Ms. Rose Ningshen and Ms. Luingamla Muinao

www.ingramcontent.com/pod-product-compliance
Ingram Content Group UK Ltd.
Pitfield, Milton Keynes, MK11 3LW, UK
UKHW020244240426